P9-CLP-389

Pope Benedict XVI

MODERN WORLD LEADERS

Tony Blair
George W. Bush
Hugo Chávez
Pope Benedict XVI
Pope John Paul II
The Saudi Royal Family
Vladimir Putin

Pope Benedict XVI

Clifford W. Mills

CHELSEA HOUSE
PUBLISHERS

An imprint of Infobase Publishing

Pope Benedict XVI

Chelsea House
An imprint of Infobase Publishing
132 West 31st Street
New York, NY 10001

Library of Congress Cataloging-in-Publication Data

Mills, Cliff, 1947–
  Pope Benedict XVI / Clifford W. Mills.
     p. cm. — (Modern world leaders)
  Includes bibliographical references and index.
  ISBN 0-7910-9228-3 (hardcover)
  1. Benedict XVI, Pope, 1927—Juvenile literature. 2. Popes—Biography—Juvenile literature. I. Title. II. Series.
  BX1378.6.M55 2006
  282.092—dc22   2006010610

Chelsea House books are available at special discounts when purchased in bulk quantities for businesses, associations, institutions, or sales promotions. Please call our Special Sales Department in New York at (212) 967-8800 or (800) 322-8755.

You can find Chelsea House on the World Wide Web at http://www.chelseahouse.com

Text design by Erik Lindstrom
Cover design by Takeshi Takahashi

Printed in the United States of America

Bang FOF 10 9 8 7 6 5 4 3 2 1

This book is printed on acid-free paper.

TABLE OF CONTENTS

ARTHUR M. SCHLESINGER, JR.

On Leadership

Leadership, it may be said, is really what makes the world go round. Love no doubt smoothes the passage; but love is a private transaction between consenting adults. Leadership is a public transaction with history. The idea of leadership affirms the capacity of individuals to move, inspire, and mobilize masses of people so that they act together in pursuit of an end. Sometimes leadership serves good purposes, sometimes bad; but whether the end is benign or evil, great leaders are those men and women who leave their personal stamp on history.

Now, the very concept of leadership implies the proposition that individuals can make a difference. This proposition has never been universally accepted. From classical times to the present day, eminent thinkers have regarded individuals as no more than the agents and pawns of larger forces, whether the gods and goddesses of the ancient world or, in the modern era, race, class, nation, the dialectic, the will of the people, the spirit of the times, history itself. Against such forces, the individual dwindles into insignificance.

So contends the thesis of historical determinism. Tolstoy's great novel *War and Peace* offers a famous statement of the case. Why, Tolstoy asked, did millions of men in the Napoleonic Wars, denying their human feelings and their common sense, move back and forth across Europe slaughtering their fellows? "The war," Tolstoy answered, "was bound to happen simply because it was bound to happen." All prior history determined it. As for leaders, they, Tolstoy said, "are but the labels that serve to give a name to an end and, like labels, they have the least possible connection with the event." The greater the leader, "the more conspicuous the inevitability and the predestination of every act he commits." The leader, said Tolstoy, is "the slave of history."

Determinism takes many forms. Marxism is the determinism of class. Nazism the determinism of race. But the idea of men and women as the slaves of history runs athwart the deepest human instincts. Rigid determinism abolishes the idea of human freedom—the assumption of free choice that underlies every move we make, every word we speak, every thought we think. It abolishes the idea of human responsibility, since it is manifestly unfair to reward or punish people for actions that are by definition beyond their control. No one can live consistently by any deterministic creed. The Marxist states prove this themselves by their extreme susceptibility to the cult of leadership.

More than that, history refutes the idea that individuals make no difference. In December 1931, a British politician crossing Fifth Avenue in New York City between 76th and 77th streets around 10:30 P.M. looked in the wrong direction and was knocked down by an automobile—a moment, he later recalled, of a man aghast, a world aglare: "I do not understand why I was not broken like an eggshell or squashed like a gooseberry." Fourteen months later an American politician, sitting in an open car in Miami, Florida, was fired on by an assassin; the man beside him was hit. Those who believe that individuals make no difference to history might well ponder whether the next two decades would have been the same had Mario Constasino's car killed Winston Churchill in 1931 and Giuseppe Zangara's bullet killed Franklin Roosevelt in 1933. Suppose, in addition, that Lenin had died of typhus in Siberia in 1895 and that Hitler had been killed on the western front in 1916. What would the twentieth century have looked like now?

For better or for worse, individuals do make a difference. "The notion that a people can run itself and its affairs anonymously," wrote the philosopher William James, "is now well known to be the silliest of absurdities. Mankind does nothing save through initiatives on the part of inventors, great or small, and imitation by the rest of us—these are the sole factors in human progress. Individuals of genius show the way, and set the patterns, which common people then adopt and follow."

Leadership, James suggests, means leadership in thought as well as in action. In the long run, leaders in thought may well make the greater difference to the world. "The ideas of economists and political philosophers, both when they are right and when they are wrong," wrote John Maynard Keynes, "are more powerful than is commonly understood. Indeed the world is ruled by little else. Practical men, who believe themselves to be quite exempt from any intellectual influences, are usually the slaves of some defunct economist. . . . The power of vested interests is vastly exaggerated compared with the gradual encroachment of ideas."

But, as Woodrow Wilson once said, "Those only are leaders of men, in the general eye, who lead in action. . . . It is at their hands that new thought gets its translation into the crude language of deeds." Leaders in thought often invent in solitude and obscurity, leaving to later generations the tasks of imitation. Leaders in action—the leaders portrayed in this series—have to be effective in their own time.

And they cannot be effective by themselves. They must act in response to the rhythms of their age. Their genius must be adapted, in a phrase from William James, "to the receptivities of the moment." Leaders are useless without followers. "There goes the mob," said the French politician, hearing a clamor in the streets. "I am their leader. I must follow them." Great leaders turn the inchoate emotions of the mob to purposes of their own. They seize on the opportunities of their time, the hopes, fears, frustrations, crises, potentialities. They succeed when events have prepared the way for them, when the community is awaiting to be aroused, when they can provide the clarifying and organizing ideas. Leadership completes the circuit between the individual and the mass and thereby alters history.

It may alter history for better or for worse. Leaders have been responsible for the most extravagant follies and most monstrous crimes that have beset suffering humanity. They have also been vital in such gains as humanity has made in individual freedom, religious and racial tolerance, social justice, and respect for human rights.

There is no sure way to tell in advance who is going to lead for good and who for evil. But a glance at the gallery of men and women in MODERN WORLD LEADERS suggests some useful tests.

One test is this: Do leaders lead by force or by persuasion? By command or by consent? Through most of history leadership was exercised by the divine right of authority. The duty of followers was to defer and to obey. "Theirs not to reason why/Theirs but to do and die." On occasion, as with the so-called enlightened despots of the eighteenth century in Europe, absolutist leadership was animated by humane purposes. More often, absolutism nourished the passion for domination, land, gold, and conquest and resulted in tyranny.

The great revolution of modern times has been the revolution of equality. "Perhaps no form of government," wrote the British historian James Bryce in his study of the United States, *The American Commonwealth*, "needs great leaders so much as democracy." The idea that all people should be equal in their legal condition has undermined the old structure of authority, hierarchy, and deference. The revolution of equality has had two contrary effects on the nature of leadership. For equality, as Alexis de Tocqueville pointed out in his great study *Democracy in America*, might mean equality in servitude as well as equality in freedom.

"I know of only two methods of establishing equality in the political world," Tocqueville wrote. "Rights must be given to every citizen, or none at all to anyone . . . save one, who is the master of all." There was no middle ground "between the sovereignty of all and the absolute power of one man." In his astonishing prediction of twentieth-century totalitarian dictatorship, Tocqueville explained how the revolution of equality could lead to the *Führerprinzip* and more terrible absolutism than the world had ever known.

But when rights are given to every citizen and the sovereignty of all is established, the problem of leadership takes a new form, becomes more exacting than ever before. It is easy to issue commands and enforce them by the rope and the stake, the concentration camp and the *gulag*. It is much harder to use argument and achievement to overcome opposition and win consent. The Founding Fathers of the United States understood the difficulty. They believed that history had given them the opportunity to decide, as Alexander Hamilton wrote in the first Federalist Paper, whether men are indeed capable of basing government on "reflection and choice, or whether they are forever destined to depend . . . on accident and force."

Government by reflection and choice called for a new style of leadership and a new quality of followership. It required leaders to be responsive to popular concerns, and it required followers to be active and informed participants in the process. Democracy does not eliminate emotion from politics; sometimes it fosters demagoguery; but it is confident that, as the greatest of democratic leaders put it, you cannot fool all of the people all of the time. It measures leadership by results and retires those who overreach or falter or fail.

It is true that in the long run despots are measured by results too. But they can postpone the day of judgment, sometimes indefinitely, and in the meantime they can do infinite harm. It is also true that democracy is no guarantee of virtue and intelligence in government, for the voice of the people is not necessarily the voice of God. But democracy, by assuring the right of opposition, offers built-in resistance to the evils inherent in absolutism. As the theologian Reinhold Niebuhr summed it up, "Man's capacity for justice makes democracy possible, but man's inclination to justice makes democracy necessary."

A second test for leadership is the end for which power is sought. When leaders have as their goal the supremacy of a master race or the promotion of totalitarian revolution or the acquisition and exploitation of colonies or the protection of greed and privilege or the preservation of personal power, it is likely that their leadership will do little to advance the cause of humanity. When their goal is the abolition of slavery, the liberation of women, the enlargement of opportunity for the poor and powerless, the extension of equal rights to racial minorities, the defense of the freedoms of expression and opposition, it is likely that their leadership will increase the sum of human liberty and welfare.

Leaders have done great harm to the world. They have also conferred great benefits. You will find both sorts in this series. Even "good" leaders must be regarded with a certain wariness. Leaders are not demigods; they put on their trousers one leg after another just like ordinary mortals. No leader is infallible, and every leader needs to be reminded of this at regular intervals. Irreverence irritates leaders but is their salvation. Unquestioning submission corrupts leaders and demeans followers. Making a cult of a leader is always a mistake. Fortunately hero worship generates its own antidote. "Every hero," said Emerson, "becomes a bore at last."

The single benefit the great leaders confer is to embolden the rest of us to live according to our own best selves, to be active, insistent, and resolute in affirming our own sense of things. For great leaders attest to the reality of human freedom against the supposed inevitabilities of history. And they attest to the wisdom and power that may lie within the most unlikely of us, which is why Abraham Lincoln remains the supreme example of great leadership. A great leader, said Emerson, exhibits new possibilities to all humanity. "We feed on genius. . . . Great men exist that there may be greater men."

Great leaders, in short, justify themselves by emancipating and empowering their followers. So humanity struggles to master its destiny, remembering with Alexis de Tocqueville: "It is true that around every man a fatal circle is traced beyond which he cannot pass; but within the wide verge of that circle he is powerful and free; as it is with man, so with communities." ●

1

Replacing a Pope for the Ages

THE WORLD CHANGED DRAMATICALLY ON SATURDAY, APRIL 2, 2005, at 9:37 P.M. Rome time. John Paul II, the second-longest serving pope in the 2,000-year history of the Catholic Church died after a lengthy illness. Hundreds of thousands of mourners gathered in Saint Peter's Square in Vatican City. Some visitors to the Vatican were startled by the powerful emotions that the popular pope's death brought to the growing crowd drawn from around the world. Some dropped to their knees on the cobblestones in the square and sobbed so violently they could not be comforted by anyone; others seemed stunned as they began their cycle of grief at the loss. Pope John Paul II had been an extraordinary presence, and his absence was overwhelming.

The search for a new pope would begin soon, according to traditions and procedures that date back centuries. But, as the print, television, and online media swarmed the Vatican, the world first needed to acknowledge the pope's death by recounting his extraordinary life.

POPE JOHN PAUL II

Karol Wojtyla was born in Wadowice, Poland, on May 18, 1920. As he grew up, his many talents and interests grew as well. He loved soccer, swimming, hiking, and skiing; he was a poet and amateur actor; he worked at several jobs, including laboring long hours in a chemical plant in Krakow. He finally found his calling in the Catholic Church, and his rise from priest to cardinal to pope was unusually rapid. When he was elected Pope John Paul II on October 16, 1978, he was only 58 years old, and he was the first non-Italian pope in 455 years.

John Paul II traveled to more countries than any pope in history (he took 104 long trips), canonized more saints, and wrote more books and letters. Some only half-joked that he was the first rock-star pope, heard and cheered by immense crowds wherever he went. He could be seen swaying to music, throwing himself into crowds, and kissing the ground whenever he walked off an airplane. He was considered a genius in handling the news media, and his training as an actor helped him reach many different kinds of audiences. Those audiences always saw a self-assured and confident leader. When American President Bill Clinton first witnessed John Paul II shaking hands in a crowd at a church in New York City, and watched normally shy and reserved nuns leap over benches to meet the pope, Clinton remarked that he would never want to have to run for office against such an effective "politician." John Paul seemed to belong to a kind of super-royalty, and his power and glory had few boundaries.

Many say John Paul II's greatest accomplishment was his role in pressuring the Soviet Union to reform: He had supported the Polish Solidarity movement against the Communists; he negotiated with Soviet leader Mikhail Gorbachev to gain some religious freedoms for those under

Communist rule; and he preached and pleaded for a non-violent moral revolution, and that revolution tore down the infamous Berlin Wall in 1989. He was considered to be a very dangerous man by some in the Soviet empire, and when an assassin shot and almost killed him in St. Peter's Square on May 13, 1981, rumors started almost immediately that the gunman had links to the Soviet police, the KGB. The rumors and suspicions continue to this day.

The new pope would clearly have a difficult time filling these shoes. But, the papacy has been one of the most visible and demanding positions for a world leader for centuries, testing each and every man who has risen to that exalted level.

THE PAPAL TRADITION

The papacy is one of the oldest institutions on earth—only the emperor of Japan can claim that his position is older. Pope John Paul II was the 262nd pope, continuing a tradition that started with St. Peter the Apostle, the leader of the original twelve disciples of Jesus Christ. Each pope is very aware that he is a direct descendent of St. Peter in the eyes of the Catholic Church, and each is addressed as "Your Holiness." St. Peter was believed to have been crucified in a marshy area on the right bank of the Tiber River in Rome. St. Peter's Basilica, the world's largest church, is built on that burial site and is one of the most important symbols of the church.

Throughout history, popes have been warriors and men of peace, scholars and diplomats, politicians and bureaucrats. They have called for crusades and wars and have negotiated peaceful alliances with other powers. Some popes were former slaves, and some former aristocrats. Some have been strong and successful leaders, and some weak and failing exiles. Only two popes have been given the title "Great" after their names (many say John Paul II will be the third): Pope Leo the Great (pope from A.D. 440 to 461) confronted a rampaging and rapacious Attila the Hun and convinced him to spare Rome.

Pope John Paul II drew stadium-size crowds on his visit to the United States in October 1979. The span of his papacy and his strong leadership style ensured that he would have a lasting impact on world history.

When the barbarians known as the Vandals later captured the city, he once again negotiated a peace and saved the people of Rome from torture and death. Pope Gregory the Great (590–604) saw Rome survive famine and plague and reached out to other churches to strengthen relationships with other faiths. He sent a delegation to England in 596 to help revive the Catholic Church there.

Many other popes have been considered to be effective leaders. Pope Innocent III (1198–1216) may have been the most powerful pope. He proclaimed that the pope had the power to overthrow kings and was inferior only to God. He instituted many reforms in the church and called for the Fourth Crusade. Pope Pius IV (1559–1565) eliminated much corruption and scandal and ushered in a golden age for the Roman Catholic Church that lasted for centuries.

Several popes have been disastrous for the church—they were the wrong men at the wrong time. Most historians agree that Pope Pius VI (1775–1799) was a vain man with a closed mind, unable to react to the changes around him. He was sent into exile by French emperor Napoleon Bonaparte, who neither feared nor respected the pope and his leadership. He died a desperate and humiliated prisoner. Several popes are remembered by history as arrogant and corrupt, and several of these in succession culminated in a revolution against them and the church's excesses and greed, led by Martin Luther. We now call this the Protestant Reformation, and the issue of the need for periodic church reform has never gone away.

THE PAPAL AUTHORITY

The pope is the supreme pontiff of the Roman Catholic Church and the head of a very large organization. During its long struggle to survive persecution and dissension from within, the Catholic Church evolved into an efficient organization that has its origins in the Roman Empire itself. The church's enduring multilayered structure is similar in many ways to that of modern large corporations and armed forces. Just as feudalism had kings, lords, vassals, and serfs in descending order of power and control, the church has the pope, cardinals, bishops, priests, and nuns. Just as corporations can delegate through CEOs, vice presidents, managers, and workers, the pope can delegate through hundreds of cardinals and some 4,200 bishops, 400,000 priests, and 1,000,000 nuns to the roughly one billion Roman Catholic Church members worldwide. His word is in some very real sense their command.

The church's strong hierarchical organization is tough and resilient, allowing for replacements to be made quickly and easily because the larger units are similar to the smaller units. It has the advantage of not fighting certain tendencies in human nature, especially the needs for order and authority. Lines of authority are clear, and rules and penalties are in writing and known to all. Like all organizations, when threatened the church closes ranks and tries to control damage, sometimes ruthlessly.

Each pope inherits a legendary bureaucracy, somewhat similar to what a U.S. president faces upon election. The church has a secretary of state and several standing committees: the Congregations for Bishops, Clergy, and Doctrine of the Faith are powerful agencies managed by church administrators, many of whom are lifelong bureaucrats. Unlike a U.S. president, the pope does not have a legal or constitutional responsibility as part of the church. He does, however, have a religious and moral authority and is in fact one of the few authorities on earth to proclaim ultimate moral values. Just as the United States has had ongoing tensions between state governments and the federal government about who has the power to do what, the Catholic Church has had a long history of tension between the pope and his authority in Rome and national and local churches that want the power to make decisions closer to home.

The pope is also a head of state, where he does have legal and political power. He rules over the Vatican, a city-state of 109 acres carved out of Rome. Some 450 people live in Vatican City permanently, and the pope has a special passport in case people are unsure of who he is when he travels. The Vatican is a unique place, containing the world's largest and most famous church, the Apostolic Palace, where the pope and several cardinals live. It also contains museums, relics, documents, books, priceless works of art, and sentimental mementos. No one knows all that is there. The Vatican's wealth, beauty, and secrecy are legendary and have survived through the ages.

THE PAPAL CANDIDATES

Very soon after the death of John Paul II, the 65 men who are part of an inner circle called the College of Cardinals met in the Sola Bologna, a large and glorious meeting room in the Apostolic Palace. All were aware of the history of the papacy, the lines of authority in the church, and the importance of what was to happen next. But before a new pope could be elected, John Paul II's funeral needed to be arranged. The dean of the College of Cardinals was a man named Joseph Ratzinger, a controversial lightning rod in the church. Ratzinger had been called Pope John Paul's "enforcer," capable of deflecting criticism from the pope by publicly defending the church's conservative positions against contraception, abortion, the ordination of women as priests, and many other issues. During the pope's long illness, Ratzinger had taken over several administrative responsibilities and had been invaluable in seeing the pope and the church through a very difficult period. Now, he took control of the funeral planning.

On April 8, 2005, Ratzinger presided over the largest funeral in history—some 2,000,000 mourners filled the streets of the Vatican and Rome all the way to the Tiber River. Some were very rich, some were very poor, and some were not even particularly Catholic or even religious. All knew they had to be part of a farewell for one of the most dynamic world leaders. Heads of state in the enormous crowd included presidents and kings; for the first time in history, a U.S. president attended a papal funeral. They heard Joseph Ratzinger give such a moving funeral speech that millions began to notice

Crowds pack St. Peter's Square at the Vatican on April 8, 2005, the day of Pope John Paul II's funeral. Kings, queens, heads of state, rich, poor, powerful, common—people from all walks of life were present to show their respect.

what Vatican insiders had known for years—that he was an articulate and forceful spokesperson for the church. Cardinal Ratzinger clearly revered the pope, but he also conveyed the deepest sorrow at losing a good friend.

Soon after John Paul's death, the cardinals of the Catholic Church who were not living in or near the Vatican began their travels to Rome, leaving Bombay, Buenos Aires, Los Angeles, Khartoum, and cities all over the world to attend the funeral. Their main goal for their long journeys, however, was to attend a special meeting called a conclave to elect the next pope. The period between the death of one pope and the election of another is called the *sede vacante*, and this interim period always has high drama both on the world stage and behind the scenes. When a pope dies, the cardinal electors can then openly discuss his replacement, something they would never do while he was still alive. Political maneuvering by papal candidates, called *papabili*, takes place very quietly during small dinners, walks around St. Peter's Square, and quick conversations over coffee. Being a candidate in a papal election is a far cry from what American political candidates experience. The "papabile" cannot present a platform and cannot even acknowledge that he is running. He can, however, maneuver quietly for votes and try to block his opponents. Successful papal candidates must be men of prayer and conscience above all else, but they must also be interested in exercising power. They must be other-worldly and worldly at the same time, and only a special few are even considered.

The cardinals knew the new pope would face one issue above all else: the decline of Christianity in Europe and the United Kingdom. They were almost certainly aware of a Gallup Millennium Survey that showed only 20 percent of Western Europeans attend church services at least once a week (in comparison, 47 percent of North Americans and 82 percent of West Africans attend weekly). The de-Christianization of Europe is relatively recent, and there are many explanations, ranging from the pessimism arising out of so many twentieth-century wars (World War II, Korean War, Vietnam War, Middle East wars) to the rise of alternatives to formal religion. Some think the Catholic Church's conservative stance on so many issues has finally alienated whole generations. The insistence that priests be celibate and that women cannot be ordained as priests certainly has turned some away from both Catholicism and from organized religion.

The cardinals were well aware that attendance at Mass has been dropping and the numbers of priests and nuns have been decreasing. They knew that liberal and reform factions in the church are constantly at odds with the conservatives who resist changes. What to do about these declines, and who best to lead the church in this divided condition, were the subjects that loomed over all else.

One papal title is Patriarch of the West, and others include Bishop of Rome and Sovereign of the State of the Vatican City. Because of this, an Italian or at least a European candidate has often been favored, reflecting the historical geographical center of the church. Cardinals from Latin America and Africa must have argued that a new geographic center for the church is emerging, one outside of Europe. Their voice and influence are growing as a group, and some media outlets speculated that the church would have its first black or Latin American pope. Some papal historians noticed that, in the past, a vigorous, outgoing, and adventurous pope like John Paul II had been followed by someone more introspective and more content to stroll through the Vatican gardens rather than climb the Alps. The serious candidates had to be published authors to prove their theological qualifications and needed to speak many languages. Since Pope John Paul II was such an important and visible world figure, the cardinals may have felt that they needed to elect an especially experienced and well-known candidate.

Gradually, the cardinals began to form coalitions around the issues that were important to them and their regions, and three front-runners emerged. (The following is only informed speculation, since nothing official is ever recorded from the conclaves and the ballots are burned in the Sistine Chapel stove.) Archbishop Carlo Maria Martini, the archbishop emeritus of Milan, became one powerful candidate. He is Italian, which is always a consideration for the electors, many of whom are from Italy. In fact, many newspapers from around the world were predicting the return of an Italian pope. He was also a progressive reformer, who would almost certainly try to bring sweeping changes to the church. He was 78 years old, as was another other front-runner, Joseph Ratzinger. Cardinal Ratzinger had impressed the world with his handling of the pope's funeral and had impressed insiders with his administration of church duties during the pope's illness. With his record of conservative values similar to John Paul's, he stood in direct opposition to Archbishop Martini. The third candidate was Cardinal Jorge Mario Bergoglio from Argentina, who was quite clear about not wanting the job. However, since roughly one-half of the world's Catholics live in Latin America, Cardinal Bergoglio had to be considered. Other candidates seemed to recede into the background, and the competition heated up very quickly. The time had come to vote.

THE ELECTION

Finally, on April 18, 2005, a procession of 115 cardinals entered St. Peter's Basilica for a special Votive Mass for the election of the pope. As dean of the College of Cardinals, Ratzinger looked out to the men in red and white sitting in semicircular rows and said:

> How many winds of doctrine we have known the recent decades, how many ideological currents, how many ways of

thinking…. The small boat of thought of many Christians has often been tossed about by these waves—thrown from one extreme to the other: from Marxism to liberalism…. from atheism to vague religious mysticism…. Having a clear faith, based on the creed of the church, is often labeled today as fundamentalism. Whereas relativism, which is letting oneself be tossed and swept along by every wind of teaching, looks like the only attitude…. We are moving toward a dictatorship of relativism which does not recognize anything as for certain. However, we have a different goal: the Son of God, true man…. In Christ, truth and love coincide…. Love without truth would be blind; truth without love would be like a resounding gong.

Several cardinals would admit later they were very moved by the power and clarity of Ratzinger's speech. The electors then went to the Sistine Chapel, in the Apostolic Palace. They sat at tables around the edge of the chamber, placing their red clerical hats in front of them. Uniformed Swiss Guards stood outside the door, as they have for centuries, guarding the pope and the Vatican.

The secret balloting began. A pope is elected by a two-thirds majority plus one vote, so in this 2005 conclave a new pope needed 77 votes to get elected. The ballots are counted under one of the most famous paintings in the world, Michelangelo's *Last Judgment*, which shows Jesus Christ ordering some souls to Heaven and some to Hell. When a candidate gets the number of votes needed, the traditional notice is for white smoke to be sent through a narrow chimney out of the chapel's roof. If no one gets the votes needed, black smoke is emitted and another vote is taken after a break.

On the afternoon of April 18, two hours after the cardinals had entered the chapel, the world saw black smoke leave the chimney. Even though a first-ballot election is rare,

Cardinals walk in procession to the Vatican's Sistine Chapel to begin the papal conclave on April 18, 2005. The cardinals were sequestered until they agreed upon a candidate to elect to the head of the Roman Catholic Church.

many of the expectant pilgrims waiting outside wept openly, bitterly disappointed and fearful that a long and bitter fight was coming. Even though the balloting is a top secret, many experts have since speculated about what was happening. Close watchers of the process thought that Archbishop Martini, Cardinal Bergoglio, and Cardinal Ratzinger split the first vote, with Ratzinger in the lead. A second ballot had Ratzinger increase his lead, and many thought the momentum was unstoppable from there. The cardinals who had not voted for him began to rethink their positions, given that a growing core was going to stick with him. Rumors about a secret meeting between Ratzinger and Martini are now

At 6:48 p.m. Rome time, a cardinal deacon proclaimed: "We have a pope!"

part of the story of this election, with many speculating on what was said. The tension was mounting, but the agonizing uncertainty was coming to an end.

The next day, April 19, on the fourth ballot, Joseph Ratzinger received a clear majority of votes. He was then asked by a group of the highest ranking and oldest cardinals whether he accepts the election to pope, and if so, what he would like his papal name to be. Ratzinger accepts, much to the relief of those hanging on his every word, and then declares that his papal name will be Benedict XVI. A Vatican journalist close to the pope, H.J. Fischer, later wrote that Ratzinger had a number of reasons for choosing the name. First, Saint Benedict was the founder of the part of the church devoted to monasticism, the practice of retreating into a safe and self-contained place to study, work, and pray. Ratzinger was a scholar at heart, and knew the importance of Saint Benedict's teachings. Also, the last pope with the name Benedict was Benedict XV, who served throughout the First World War and tried to remain neutral and pacifying under the most difficult conditions. He helped reunite Europe after that first global conflict ended. Benedict XV had a pivotal healing role, at least temporarily, one that Ratzinger must have admired. Finally, the word Benedict derives from the Latin "benedictus," which means blessed, and surely Ratzinger hoped to be blessed in his time as pope. It was a Latin word he had heard all his life sung during Mass, and the very sound of it must have pleased and comforted him.

At 6:48 p.m. Rome time, a cardinal deacon proclaimed: "We have a pope!" Because of some fault in the chimney, gray smoke at first appeared above the Sistine Chapel, confusing

White smoke is released from the Sistine Chapel chimney on April 19, 2005, signaling the election of Pope Benedict XVI. Although there was much deliberation, the conclave was one of the shortest in history.

many below. Then the Vatican bells start ringing, and whiter smoke began to float out. Now the world knew a new pope was about to step forth onto the central balcony overlooking St. Peter's Square. Joseph Ratzinger, now the Holy Father and Pope Benedict XVI, appeared dressed in a white cassock and skullcap, wrapped in a red and gold cape, and opened his arms to the world.

His first words to the crowd below were, "Dear brothers and sisters, after the great pope John Paul II, the cardinals have elected me, a simple and humble worker in the Lord's vineyard." The people below began to chant "Viva Il Papa," "Long live the pope!" Many waved flags, from all countries. Stores closed, celebrations began, and drivers honked horns so incessantly that camera crews had trouble with their

No longer known as Joseph Ratzinger, newly elected Pope Benedict XVI waves to the crowd from the balcony of St. Peter's Basilica at the Vatican on April 19, 2005.

sound systems. Gridlock hit Rome, not for the first time, and not for the last. An instant holiday was in full swing.

FIRST IMPRESSIONS

Some experts and faithful followers from around the world were surprised or skeptical at the election. Ratzinger is German, and no German has been elected pope in almost 500 years. He is a conservative. He is unusually humble and reserved, and not flamboyant—Vatican residents had become used to seeing him walk to work with a tattered black briefcase and informal clothing. He didn't seem to want to be pope, dismissing the idea publicly many times—he said he would rather be guillotined. He had hoped he could retire. But Pope John Paul II had believed in him and promoted him quickly. All saw his skill at speaking and his command of five languages (German, French, Italian, English, and Spanish). He can read old Greek, Latin, and classical Hebrew. He is clearly a brilliant intellectual, an academic dedicated to interpreting words. He has a near-photographic memory as well as encyclopedic knowledge. All who had seen him celebrate Mass commented on the delicacy and devotion that he brings to it, and his loving eulogy for John Paul II filled many cardinals with affection for him. He would be a dramatic change from John Paul II, but some were looking forward to a less hectic papacy.

Barely twelve hours after his election, Pope Benedict made his first formal speech as pope, addressing the cardinals in the Sistine Chapel:

> I consider this a grace obtained for me by my venerated predecessor, John Paul II. It seems I can feel his strong hand squeezing mine; I seem to see his smiling eyes and listen to his words, addressed to me especially at this moment: "Do not be afraid!" ... I address myself to everyone, even those who follow other religions or who are simply seeking an answer to the fundamental questions of life and have not found it yet.... I am particularly thinking of young people.

He must have stopped at some point in those first few days as pope and reflected on just how far he had come from a very small town in Bavaria, Germany.

2

Growing up in Paradise

THE MAN WHO WOULD BECOME POPE BENEDICT XVI WAS BORN IN RURAL southern Bavaria, Germany, on April 16, 1927. Joseph Ratzinger came into the world on an exceptionally cold morning for spring, at 4:15 A.M. His parents, Joseph and Maria, were so worried about the cold that they didn't bring his brother, Georg, or sister, Maria, to his baptism later that day. April 16 was Holy Saturday, the day after Good Friday and before Easter Sunday, and Ratzinger would later think this was an important sign in his life. Some have suggested that having parents named Joseph and Mary (the more familiar form for "Maria") could only have struck him as another auspicious sign as well.

Ratzinger's father was a police officer and police supervisor, or *gendarmerie-kommissar*. He was a civil servant and so was protected from much of the economic uncertainty that Germany faced after World War I. Unlike many others around him, his income didn't fluctuate with farm prices or business downturns. Pictures show him to be an impressively handsome man with a well-trimmed mustache and with a confident and direct gaze into the camera. He was known for his integrity. When a new political party began to spy on and then bully citizens, he tried to warn and protect those he could. The party became known as the Nazis, and one of their enemies was Joseph Ratzinger, Sr.

Ratzinger's mother was a professional cook before she married, working in the bustling city of Munich. She specialized as a dessert chef, and her son Joseph would later write about the family's love of her cooking. She was a small and vibrant woman with strong facial features.

In his autobiography, *Milestones*, Ratzinger recalls his parents with an obvious love that didn't diminish as he grew. He says he inherited his father's "critical mind" and his mother's "warm-hearted religious sense." Throughout his education, he would constantly draw on and cultivate both the analytical and the religious sides of his personality. His fate was to be analytical about religion.

Joseph and Maria had married in 1920 and wasted little time in starting a family. Maria, their first child, was born in 1921, and their first son, Georg, was born in 1924. The future pope was especially close with his two siblings—his sister Maria was six years older and seems to have looked after her baby brother in every way. Georg had a number of interests that his younger brother picked up, including a love of music. Georg was the friendly jokester of the family, the most outgoing. The third child in a family of three often has a special sense of privilege and entitlement, and we can assume that this family had some of that well-known birth-order dynamic.

The family was neither rich nor poor. They did everything together, or at least tried. Gathering each day for the family dinner seems to have been an especially close time. This was a happy, religious, and secure family, residing in one of the most beautiful

This photo of the Raztinger family dates from 1938. Pictured from left are: Joseph, brother Georg, mother Maria, sister Maria, and father Joseph.

parts of the world. Joseph Ratzinger and his brother and sister were living in something very close to a child's paradise.

BAVARIA

Growing up in Bavaria had a profound effect on Ratzinger, and in his autobiography he spends many more pages recalling his childhood there than he does any other time in his long life. Bavaria is the largest state within Germany, and also the most rural. Almost half of its people still live in towns of fewer than 6,000 residents. It has had its own military, postal system, and railways. Deep forests, high mountains, and strong rivers define the landscape that is still today a world destination for tourism and outdoor recreation. Because it is at the foot of the Alps, it has some of the most extreme weather in Europe.

Bavaria became officially a Catholic state in the sixteenth century when its king opposed the Protestant Reformation.

Almost anywhere you go in Bavaria there is a Catholic church or shrine, a reflection of the weaving of the church into every community. The social and political conservatism of Bavaria goes hand in hand with its Christian faith and belief in family integrity and personal discipline. Many have compared it to the American Midwest in its political and social outlook.

In a country as diverse as the United States in the twenty-first century, it is hard to imagine the kind of uniform and homogeneous culture Bavaria experienced in the nineteenth and early twentieth centuries, but almost every village, town, and city had a town square with decorated shop windows and beautiful two- and three-story houses with tile roofs surrounding the town focus—the local Catholic church. Some have described this kind of village life as being in a life-size snow globe, clean and neat. Life in a Bavarian village is to this day a very regular and regulated process. Crops cannot be planted without authorization from the regional agricultural office; even minor work on a home in the village requires permission from the local officials. Regulations restrict freedoms but allow for a surface harmony and planned attractiveness that continue to characterize the region. Growing up in such ordered beauty and such a secure homeland could easily have made a sensitive and impressionable child think that such a joyful creation was evidence of a benevolent creator.

Ratzinger's family stayed in one section of Bavaria throughout his childhood, the area between the Inn and Salzach rivers. But they moved four times in his first ten years. He opens his autobiography by saying it is not easy to note which is his hometown, so he belongs to a region more than any one town.

The first village they lived in as a family is named Marktl am Inn, which is on the border with Austria in the southeastern corner of Germany. The Ratzingers occupied the second floor in a large, white three-story wooden house. Ratzinger's first memory is from here: A dentist lived on the first floor and was the first in the area to get a motorcar, a relative rarity

Joseph Ratzinger's birthplace in Marktl, Germany, is photographed as it appears today. Ratzinger lived in Marktl for the first two years of his life.

in the late 1920s in Bavaria. Ratzinger remembers the smell of the gasoline.

In 1929, when Joseph was two, the family moved to the town of Tittmoning, a slightly larger village with a current population of 5,600. Another of his first and strongest early memories is of the Ponlach Chapel, high on a steep hillside overlooking the town. Ratzinger writes of his complete happiness roaming the lush fields around the town and bringing back flowers and other things from nature for his family.

On a sunny spring day in 1932, a black limousine pulled into the village square. Cardinal Michael Faulhaber, the archbishop of Munich, stepped out to a great welcoming party of small children. He was a towering figure to them, made more impressive by his princely robes. Ratzinger was dazzled by the spectacle and came home and announced, "I want to be a cardinal." Many think his path to the papacy began at that moment.

His third hometown was Aschau am Inn. This village is famed as one of the most beautiful small villages in all of Bavaria, and in all the world. It is a real-life fantasyland, with stunning views of the twelfth-century Hohenaschau castle, which looks down into the Prien Valley. The Bavarian Alps provide a perfect scenic backdrop. The village's church, with magnificent towers and spectacular gold-trimmed paintings on its ceiling, remains a tourist attraction. Today, the village is primarily a health and ski resort, with a large nature preserve nearby frequented by ecotourists.

The Ratzingers lived in an old country farmhouse. A small pond filled with carp watered the flowered meadow behind the house. The scene gave the family many hours of pleasure during long walks and hikes. Only two events seem to have threatened their peaceful and contented lives here. One was when young Joseph nearly drowned in the pond while playing at its edge. The other was the construction of a new building, a lighthouse built on one of the hills surrounding the village. Why would a lighthouse have been needed in the mountains? No one could know for sure at the time, but being able to detect airplanes at night would soon be very important. Charles Lindbergh had brought the world's attention to air travel when he flew across the Atlantic a few years before, and German military planners quickly saw uses for the airplane other than travel. Ratzinger writes that the lighthouse's light "appeared like a flash of lightning announcing a danger that still had no name.... We vaguely perceived that what was being prepared could only be reason for deep concern; but, in a world apparently at total peace, no one could believe something sinister."

The last of Ratzinger's childhood hometowns was Traunstein, a bigger city of some 11,000 people. In 1937, the family moved to a section of the city called Hufschlag, into an old farmhouse his father had bought in 1933 for when he retired. At the age of 60, Ratzinger's father now left the police force and spent a good deal of his new retirement time fixing up the old house, helped by each member of the family. The date of 1726 was inscribed in one of the beams, so apparently a good deal of work was needed. There was no running water, but just outside the house was an orchard, with cherry, apple, pear, and plum trees. On one side, an endless pine forest extended into darkness. On the other side was a meadow filled with primroses in the spring. Several outbuildings, especially a shadowy weaving shed, provided mystery as the children explored them. As with the other three towns, this was again an idyllic place to grow up.

EARLY EDUCATION, EARLY FAITH

Until moving to Traunstein, Ratzinger had been homeschooled. Now, at the age of 10, he walked a half hour to a school in the center of the city, a school called a *gymnasium*. These kinds of schools in Germany at the time specialized in classical Greek and Latin studies, and Ratzinger was immediately drawn in by the rigorous work. He read and memorized not only some of the classics, but also works by some of the famous German writers, such as Goethe. He enjoyed his schoolwork and began to look forward to losing himself in great literature.

In 1939, Ratzinger followed an instinct he had for some time, at least since he was five: He decided to be a priest. He entered the minor seminary at Traunstein, named Saint Michael Seminary, where he now had to live. He hated being away from home and missed his family terribly. He had grown used to studying next to Georg and Maria. He had built a childhood world of his own, and now his world had many more people living in it. Sitting and studying with 60 other

Photographed in 2005, St. Michael's Seminary in Traunstein, Germany, was Joseph Ratzinger's first home away from home and was the site of his 1951 ordination.

students was especially difficult for him. There was one other factor in his dislike of school:

> If this became such complete torture for me, it was because I am not at all gifted at sports and also because I was the youngest of all the boys, some of whom were as much as three years older than I. Thus, I was inferior to most in physical strength.... In the long run, it is not very pleasant to have to live on others' tolerance, knowing that you are nothing but a burden for the team to which you are assigned.

Ratzinger discovered that one thing gave him comfort among the difficulties of being away from home and not being athletic or popular: that one thing was the life and feelings he found when he was in church. He writes that "life without the

Adolf Hitler (right) rides in a motorcade with Italian dictator Benito Mussolini in Munich, Germany, in 1940. Hitler's rise to power impacted the life of Joseph Ratzinger profoundly.

church would have simply fallen into the void." At this age he was more aware of the mysterious world of the Catholic liturgy, "the tapestry of texts and actions that had developed over centuries." His father and mother were devout Catholics, and he had grown up going to church regularly. It was one of the things the family always did together. Early on he had felt a trust in God that "penetrated deeply into my soul." He loved the public life of the church, the complex, moving services in which every gesture and word had some special meaning. He found it all a kind of medieval castle of Latin song and prayer, fragrant incense and ancient sacraments. He loved exploring it and being protected by it.

As the seasons changed, so did the church's holidays. "I can still smell those carpets of flowers.... I can see all the houses decorated, the banners, the singing; I can still hear the village band." Lent became Easter, which gave way to Pentecost, and then Christmas. Throughout his young life, Ratzinger lived in the seasons of the church as much as he lived in the seasons of nature.

In Germany at this time, an education almost always included musical instruction. While in Traunstein, both Ratzinger brothers would travel to the nearby city of Salzburg, Austria, just across the Salzach River. When they heard performances of Beethoven's Ninth Symphony, and Mozart's Mass in C Minor, they were captured by music for the rest of their lives. For many years, Ratzinger tried to play the piano every day, preferring Mozart and Beethoven to all others. Both boys burrowed into books and music, turning inward from the world that was about to break on them.

Gradually, Joseph Senior and his two sons began to listen less and less to music on the radio, and more to news. The Allied (alliance of the United States, United Kingdom, France, and others) radio broadcasts, they began to realize, were very different from that of the German news they were hearing. Joseph Senior had long been trying to warn his family, friends, and colleagues about the new rising political power, the National Socialists, or Nazi (from the German word *Nationalsozialist*) Party. The party was led by a man named Adolf Hitler, and Joseph Senior saw more clearly than most that Hitler would lead Germany into war, destruction, and chaos. He helped warn people when they were about to be investigated by this new ruling party, and now his warnings were taking on a new urgency. Few seemed to be listening. A serpent had taken over the Garden of Eden that the Ratzinger children had lived in, and its poisonous bite began to kill.

3

Paradise Lost

ON THE NIGHT OF NOVEMBER 9, 1938, ROVING MOBS ATTACKED THE HOUSES of each of the Jewish citizens living in Traunstein and many other German cities. Wearing brown shirts, the terrorists escalated Nazi violence to a new level. In Traunstein, they smashed windows and threatened the Jewish families with a choice of either leaving or being killed. The night came to be called *Kristallnacht*, or "the Night of the Broken Glass." Throughout Germany, hundreds of Jews were killed and injured, and thousands of businesses were destroyed. Some consider that night to be the beginning of what is now known at the Holocaust.

The most prominent Jewish family in Traunstein was the Holzer family. They decided to leave the next day and moved to Munich. Three years later, they would be sent to a concentration camp, Dachau, and all would die except for a young daughter. Another of Traunstein's citizens, Rosa Mousbauer, drowned herself after that night rather than be forced to

A pedestrian looks at a vandalized Jewish-owned shop in Berlin on November 10, 1938, the day after Kristallnacht, or "the night of broken glass." On that night, Nazis vandalized and looted Jewish businesses and places of worship, and attacked Jews in Germany and Austria.

leave. On November 12, 1938, a Nazi regional leader declared Traunstein "free of Jews."

Joseph Ratzinger has never written about these times in Traunstein, and perhaps the pain and guilt of being alive during of one of the most traumatic periods in human history forced his memory to repress these events. This period, known in Germany as the Third Reich, coincided with his becoming a young man. He had to either give in to the strong currents of German events or fight against them.

THE THIRD REICH

Adolf Hitler was born in 1889 in the Austrian town of Braunau. He moved to Vienna in the hope of becoming an artist and lived in relative poverty for years as he struggled and failed at whatever he did. He joined the German army at the beginning of World War I, in 1914, and served until the war ended in 1918. He had been certain the German army would be victorious and was devastated when it wasn't. He remained in Germany, and as a corporal in the army, he was sent to spy on a new political party, the German Worker's Party. He liked the party's message of a new reborn Germany being possible, and he joined it in 1919. He helped rename the party the Nazis and became its chair in July 1921, when any opposition he faced for leadership found themselves intimidated in various ways. The party was based in Bavaria almost exclusively.

Hitler immediately radicalized the party and began to try to intimidate other political parties who opposed his Nazis. Traditional political parties had been weakened after World War I and by the economic conditions in Germany following the war. Hitler's Nazi Party promised better days in Germany, similar to the days experienced before the war. He would make more jobs available and bring back pride in being a full-blooded patriotic German. He appealed to nostalgia and promised to be a strong and decisive leader, pushing aggressively for German interests around the world. Unsuccessful in winning any elections, the party tried in 1923 to violently overthrow the Bavarian government and was crushed in two days by the government in Munich. Hitler was convicted of treason and served time in prison until 1925.

The publicity created by his imprisonments, and by the book he wrote in prison, *Mein Kampf*, helped Hitler become known outside of Bavaria, and his Nazi message spread to the rest of the country. He created a protection force called the Schutzstaffel (known as the SS), and their intimidating scare tactics moved aside much of his political opposition. Hitler also took advantage of the deeply divided and weakened traditional political parties in Germany as he made the Nazi Party a dominant force.

He became chancellor on January 30, 1933, shortly after being made a German citizen. (He had denounced his Austrian citizenship in 1925.) He moved quickly to consolidate power and crush other political parties. In March 1933, his government passed the Enabling Act, which allowed him to make his own laws. In May, labor unions were abolished. In July, other political parties were abolished. Only the Nazis remained. The German government and the Nazi Party became one and the same. Hitler felt that Germany needed only one party; he seemed to not want to govern as much as he wanted to defeat his political opponents.

The media was now controlled by the Nazi Party, and the idea of fair and balanced radio and newspaper coverage became a mockery. He saw to it that enormous amounts of money were being allocated to the military. Hitler led Germany out of high unemployment by creating thousands of jobs in and supporting the German military, and he took advantage of an improving world economic picture as the 1930s went on.

With such complete power residing with one man, his personal prejudices could now become public policy. Hitler's twisted anti-Semitism was not a secret. At first, Jewish citizens were only banned from public parks. Then they were banned from certain professions; civil servants had to be non-Jewish. Then, they were actively harassed wherever they went. The progression of prejudice was calculated and patient. In the town of Tittmoning, where the Ratzingers had lived, a prison facility was being filled with a new kind of criminal—people who questioned the Nazi Party. Reports came to the town of people dying suddenly there, but few wanted to look into what was happening. People became obedient rather than questioning, and Hitler seemed to be a strong leader, a man in charge.

CATHOLICISM DURING THE THIRD REICH

Neither the Ratzingers nor anyone they knew well were members of the Nazi Party. They opposed the Third Reich but did not become part of the small active resistance that spread anti-Nazi leaflets or disabled Nazi vehicles. Joseph Ratzinger, Sr.

tried to help those being hurt, but he and his wife, like many parents, tried to protect their children from a growing danger, and the family retreated into their rural lives. They wanted to ignore what was happening in the national government, perhaps thinking that all politics really is local. Their ignoring the situation, and the ignorance of many other citizens, would prove to be a disastrous mistake.

Pope Pius XI was the leader of the Catholic Church during the 1930s. Like many popes before, he attempted to negotiate with the threatening powers around him. He succeeded at first, gaining some protections for Catholic schools and churches. Hitler would leave the church alone if the church would not move against him and his policies of anti-Semitism. The pope felt that the Communists in Germany were a bigger threat to the country than the Nazis, and Hitler feared the Communists as well. The upper classes in Germany were also more worried about workers rising up and demanding more pay and privileges, so they tolerated the new Nazi Party, which seemed to be protecting their interests. The pope must have reasoned that the enemy of his enemy was his friend, or at least his temporary ally. Some historians feel that the Catholic Church could have stopped Hitler early on and that it was the only authority powerful enough to defeat the Nazis inside Germany. Others feel Hitler was unstoppable by a nonmilitary force. We will never know.

Many Catholic priests and nuns refused to condone the pope's cooperation with Hitler and actively fought the Third Reich. Some Catholic newspapers refused to print the lies the government told them. Some priests and nuns refused to turn away Jewish citizens who were physically and emotionally battered. By the beginning of World War II in 1939, however, some of these true Christians were being fed to the Nazi lions. Many were criminalized and imprisoned. By the end of the war, in 1945, more than 1,000 Catholic priests had been killed at the concentration camp Dachau. History has lost count of the number of nuns killed, but there were many more nuns than priests in Germany during the 1930s.

Some bishops, priests, and nuns followed the pope's leadership and did not oppose the Nazis. Some even supported Hitler openly and cooperated by giving the Nazis their church birth records (to see who was Jewish and who was not), information about families, and financial support. They tolerated and even encouraged anti-Semitism. The same Cardinal Faulhaber who had dazzled young Joseph seven years earlier was accused of collaborating with the Nazis. The Catholic Church has had to wrestle with its conscience for many years since the war and has tried to understand how it could have collectively failed to stop Hitler. Ratzinger has not publicly used his famous reasoning skills to try to help with this problem. We can only assume he has struggled to find answers.

JOSEPH RATZINGER DURING THE WAR

After Hitler conquered Poland in 1939, German citizens experienced an eerie quiet. The world appeared to be confused about what had happened. World leaders did not seem to know what to do. By 1940, Hitler's armies occupied Denmark, Norway, Holland, Belgium, and France. Some Germans felt a surge of patriotism. Just as he promised, their leader had brought pride back to many in the country, or at least had elicited fear from other countries. These people were multiplying Hitler's evil by supporting him. Ratzinger writes in his autobiography that his father "saw that a victory of Hitler's would not be a victory for Germany but rather a victory for the anti-Christ that would surely usher in apocalyptic times for all believers."

At first the war seemed unreal to Ratzinger. Then, the Soviet Union was attacked and soon huge transport trucks began rolling though Traunstein, carrying horribly wounded soldiers. Every available space became a military hospital, including the seminary where Ratzinger studied. Sent home, he returned to his old school in Traunstein. When he read each day the names of dead soldiers, some of them older friends or friends of Maria and Georg, he became depressed.

In the summer of 1942, Georg was drafted and became a signal corps operator. Sadly, one of Ratzinger's most comforting presences was now gone. At the same time, membership in the Hitler Youth became mandatory for all young men. Ratzinger was required to attend their meetings. He attended a few but refused to carry his Hitler Youth certificate and risked being severely punished for this. Fortunately, forgiving and protective teachers at his Traunstein school did not turn him in to authorities. The Hitler Youth was a training organization for the infamous SS, and there is evidence that Ratzinger was mocked and insulted for not being a good Hitler Youth. Ruling groups of all ages put intense pressure on others to conform, and Ratzinger did not conform. His depression deepened.

The most spirit-lifting and healing act for him at that point was prayer, a "retreat to the boundless realm of the spirit." Many psychologists and others have noted that when people cannot physically run from very threatening situations, they tend to retreat internally, to an inner world that seems safer. They shut off outside noises and sights and avoid a terrifying reality by entering a world of their imagination. For Ratzinger, the world of the Catholic faith and rituals, and of the family's celebration of religious feasts, became more real than they ever had. One other activity helped him through this most traumatic time: writing. He began to write seriously for the first time in his life, recording events both large and small in his journal. He found, like many before and since, that writing can reduce or at least distance pain.

In 1943, those in the seminary born in 1926 and 1927 were drafted into the German army, at the ages of 16 and 17. Ratzinger was sent to Munich to become part of an anti-aircraft defense system, called the Flak. He began training alongside other young seminarians. The students were allowed to continue with some of their classes but lived in barracks with

Joseph Ratzinger poses in uniform in this 1943 photo. Ratzinger was drafted into the German anti-aircraft defense system. Although he did not enjoy the experience, his world was broadened by it.

RATZINGER WROTE LATER THAT HE WAS LIVING IN AN "INFERNO" AND WONDERED WHETHER HE WOULD LIVE MUCH LONGER. HIS LIFE HAD REACHED ONE OF ITS LOWEST POINTS.

regular soldiers. Ratzinger was now pulled out of his beloved countryside for the first time and thrown in with many different kinds of people of many ages. Political scientists have noted that one of the most democratic forces in the world is a drafted army, where all classes and ages mix and work together toward a common goal. This force seems to have worked on 16-year-old Joseph. He realized how different he was from those not in the seminary and from those who grew up in big cities. He realized how fortunate he had been to grow up in his Bavarian paradise; city people seemed very different to him. He met older men torn from their wives and children and felt a special sympathy for them. He vowed to himself that he would learn from the experience and from the people. He longed for home, but he also vowed he would draw on some inner strength and survive whatever would be thrown at him.

After training in Munich, his anti-aircraft squad was assigned to protect the Bavarian Motor Works (BMW) north of Munich, which was making truck and airplane engines. Some of the workers there were slaves from concentration camps. Soon after, he was sent to Innsbruck, Austria, to protect a railroad station, and then to Gilching, to protect an airfield. There his battery was attacked, and one of the soldiers with him was killed and another wounded. In the summer of 1944, Munich came under vicious Allied bombings, and each time Ratzinger was sent to the city that summer, he saw that more and more of it had been destroyed. The air was constantly filled with smoke, and fires burned everywhere. He wrote later that he was living in an "inferno" and wondered whether he would live much longer. His life had reached one of its lowest points. A man who would become one of the world's most powerful leaders was one of its most powerless followers during this period in the war.

In Gilching, he sought comfort from the church, amid the war's chaos. After meeting people who were organizing Catholic services, he took part in a crude form of the elaborate rituals he grew up with and loved. His only protection was his faith. Neither family nor friends could be there for him now.

Through all this military service, Ratzinger writes in his autobiography, he never once fired a shot. He was too sick with an infection for some of the duty to be assigned to an anti-aircraft gun. We can speculate that he may not have been strong enough or an accurate enough shot to have been entrusted to one of the big cannons. He has also refused to master the art of killing.

On September 10, 1944, Ratzinger was released from the anti-aircraft unit, but he was then immediately assigned regular military duty. His job now was a backbreaking one: He and his unit were sent to Burgenland, near the border with Austria, Czechoslovakia, and Hungary, to dig long and deep trenches to trap tanks. The German high command was searching for any way to slow the Allied tanks as they swept across Europe toward Germany. This job was essentially like prison labor, and at the end of each day he tumbled to the ground exhausted. He wrote later that he was surrounded by "fanatical ideologues who tyrannized us." Once again, SS recruiters tried to get workers to join them. Once again, Ratzinger said he wanted to be a priest and was abused and mocked. The darkest period in his life was nearing an end, but first he had to undergo several more ordeals before the war was over.

At first, the forced laborers had to put away their shovels each night in spotless condition, without even a speck of dust on them. Gradually, as the months dragged on and the morale

A transport of Hungarian Jews is processed at the Auschwitz-Birkenau concentration camp in Poland in May 1944. One of three main SS-run camps, Auschwitz-Birkenau was the site of extermination for at least 1.1 million Jews; 75,000 Poles; and 19,000 Roma, or gypsies.

of the German units fell with more defeats on the battlefield, the officers in charge no longer shouted about the shovels. It was that tiny change that made Ratzinger realize the war effort was going to fail and that the Allied forces were going to defeat the German machine.

Each day he had watched Hungarian Jews being shipped to the concentration camp at Auschwitz, and each day he must have tried to hide the knowledge from himself about what was happening. By the end of the war, some 620,000 Hungarian Jews were murdered at Auschwitz. Watching the prisoners may have triggered his next actions.

Ratzinger reached a kind of moral crisis: He could no longer play any role in the carnage, and in May 1945, he deserted his unit. Instinctively, he headed for home and his parents. Even though he knew all the back roads to his home, he was in danger because soldiers had orders to shoot deserters on sight. As he emerged from a railroad underpass near his home, he saw two soldiers waiting for him. It is a moment in his life that he will never forget. For no explainable reason, they let him pass. Perhaps they too were no longer capable of murder in cold blood. Perhaps they suddenly knew the futility of their orders. Joseph Ratzinger was not yet meant to die.

He reached his home, only to find two SS officers waiting for him. They had been hanging deserters from trees outside Traunstein, as a warning to all that the Nazis were still in power. These same SS officers may have been among the ones who lined up 62 people in a field near the Ratzinger house on May 2 and shot them with machine guns. Once again, "a special angel seemed to be guarding" him, he would later write. The officers left his home without taking any action, restrained by some unseen force.

Ratzinger's troubles were not over, even though the war was in its last days. American forces arrived in Traunstein soon after the SS left and used the Ratzinger farmhouse as their headquarters for the region. The American officers told him to put his uniform back on and line up with others in the meadow behind the house. Ratzinger thought he might be executed, but just as he was leaving his house he took two things with him: a notebook and a pencil. Whatever was to happen to him, he wanted to write about it if he could. Instead of being executed, he was made a prisoner of war by the Americans. He and the others in the meadow were marched down abandoned roads toward an unknown destination. For weeks they slept in open fields,

The Ulm Cathedral had a major impact on Joseph Ratzinger. The Gothic cathedral is the tallest in the world and houses many important works of art.

with a daily spoonful of soup and a piece of bread to sustain them. They were marched to the city of Ulm, and Ratzinger says that when he saw the cathedral there untouched by the war, "the sight of it was for me like a consoling proclamation of the indestructible humaneness of faith." The prisoners were fenced in by barbed wire, and rumors swept through the camp of what was about to happen to them. The uncertainty of their fate continued until mid-June, when one by one the prisoners were released. They were released in order of their occupations. Farmers were released first; many claimed to be farmers.

On June 19, 1945, Ratzinger was sent out of the POW camp and tried to hitchhike home. A dairy truck driver stopped, asked where he was going, and laughed when Ratzinger said he was going to Traunstein. The trucker was also going to Traunstein, some 80 miles away. Finally headed home, the war was over for him. His words describe his feelings:

> I arrived in my home city even before sunset; the heavenly Jerusalem itself could not have appeared more beautiful to me at that moment. I heard praying and singing coming from the church…. I rushed home as fast as I could. My father could hardly believe it as I suddenly stood there before him, alive and well…. In my whole life I have never again had so magnificent a meal as the simple one that Mother had prepared for me from the vegetables of her own garden…. The months that followed were full of a sense of newly won freedom, something we were only now learning to treasure, and this period belongs to the most beautiful memories of my entire life.

A Paradise Regained

WORLD WAR II HAUNTED AND CONTINUES TO HAUNT GERMANY. THE ENTIRE society was traumatized by Nazism. The guilt and shame that followed changed virtually every German who survived the war. An entire culture had broken down, and many were unable to even acknowledge the depth of their own suffering. A society had to come to terms with the consequences of blind obedience to a leader. Blind obedience can unfortunately be a part of human nature, but we all learn that what is natural is not always right.

BECOMING CIVILIZED AGAIN

The war and the Nazis had destroyed many universities and seminaries. Books were hard to find. In some sense, a whole society had to start from scratch to put back together an educational life. The slow return of civilization started for Ratzinger when he enrolled at a seminary in the city of Freising, near Munich, during the winter of 1946. He and his fellow seminarians felt as if they had been at the gates of hell, and by surviving they had assumed a special responsibility to cherish life and living. The war had killed rich and poor, strong and weak, Jews and Christians, atheists and the devout. But it had not killed the 120 men arriving at Freising, ranging in age from 19 to 49, who now chose to become priests. The Catholic Church had survived, and so had they.

On September 1, 1947, Ratzinger changed schools, and went to the University of Munich Theological Institute for an education in academic theology. The university was in ruins, so students were sent to an old castle, once the royal hunting lodge of insane King Otto. Ratzinger woke up on his first night there, in his bunk bed, fearing he was somehow still at war. The students had little food and heat, and they were forced to return to their homes from Christmas to Easter. When school was in session, the students attended lectures in an old greenhouse, which meant they were usually freezing or roasting. However, there was a beautiful park surrounding the castle, and it provided a wonderful retreat for students needing a place to study and pray, as well as to think.

Some of the brightest students in all of Germany came to the institute, as did some of the best faculty. Theology teachers with backgrounds in mathematics, comparative religion, and philosophy could meet and exchange ideas. Perhaps the best known figure was Friedrich Wilhelm Maier, who had shocked the religious world by proposing that we didn't know as much as we thought about the Bible, especially the gospels by Matthew, Mark, Luke, and John. Everyone had always assumed the gospels were written in that order, with Matthew first and the others following. Using various kinds of historical and textual analysis, Maier said the gospel by Mark was written first and was the source for Matthew and Luke. A long-lost collection of the sayings of Jesus Christ was also the basis for the gospels after Mark. This is now an accepted fact by biblical scholars, but it was considered a horrible blasphemy in the

1940s. After being taught by Maier, Ratzinger writes, "the Bible spoke to us with a new immediacy and freshness."

This period served as a great awakening for Joseph Ratzinger. During this time, he read everything he could, from a wide range of disciplines. He devoured works by Russian author Fyodor Dostoevsky. Ratzinger read Friedrich Nietzsche, who famously said "God is dead." Nietzsche described the birth of a Superman who would replace God. Ratzinger read Sigmund Freud, who seemed to have the feeling that if God wasn't dead, rational and scientific people should kill him. For Freud, God was an illusion, a device of the unconscious. Although Ratzinger would later reject these thinkers, he examined their philosophies first. He read about Albert Einstein and the work in a new kind of physics, which demonstrated that events are unpredictable at the very smallest and largest levels, overthrowing the classical model that all things could be predicted if only enough data were available. There was very little room for God in classical physics, but not so in the modern physics, theologians speculated. For Ratzinger, the sciences had reopened a door to an assumption about the possible or probable existence of God. He felt that theology could ask bold new questions, just as science was asking. The church came alive to him in new ways, as did the "conservative" and "liberal/reformer" issues in the church about what needed to be kept and what needed to be replaced in Catholic traditions. Which traditions bring us closer to others, and which separate us? What could we trust, and what could we not trust? What was obsolete and what was not? Ratzinger looked for answers with a voracious energy and passion that set him apart from almost all other students.

LIFE AS A PRIEST

This wonderful period of his education finally culminated in Ratzinger becoming a priest. He was ordained on June 29, 1951, by Cardinal Michael Faulhaber, the same person he met coming out of a limousine when he was only five. The elaborate ceremony with the Sacrament of the Holy Orders took place in Freising Cathedral and was exactly the same ritual of ordination that has been practiced for centuries. Becoming a priest fulfilled one of Ratzinger's life goals. It was one of the best days of his life.

In Bavaria, a priest's first Mass is a cause for celebration and rejoicing. Ratzinger performed his first Mass in his home village of Hufschlag in the parish church of St. Oswald. The night before, nearly a thousand people poured into the village to help mark the occasion. Lights all over the village pointed the way to the Ratzinger house, and the Catholic Youth of Traunstein sang beneath the bright summer stars. Few had seen the village so bright at night when fireworks and cannons' flashes also lit the sky.

On Sunday, July 8, 1951, he celebrated his first Mass and gave his first sermon. He decided to outline his tasks as a priest: He wanted to bless, preach, baptize, and offer sacrifice. For him, the church always came to life during the liturgy, and he trusted the experience of the church and its rituals to bring people together and closer to a spiritual life. He wanted to be the vehicle through which Jesus Christ touched others. His first Mass card was reproduced in the local paper: "We aim not to lord over your faith, but to serve over your joy" (from Paul's Second Letter to the Corinthians, 1:21).

On August 1, 1951, Ratzinger started his first assignment as a priest, becoming the assistant pastor of the Church of the Precious Blood in Munich. The church was located in a suburb of Munich, in an interesting neighborhood filled with artists, intellectuals, and students. New priests take on an enormous workload, and he was no exception. Each week, he heard countless confessions; performed two Sunday masses; taught schoolchildren all week; presided over burials, weddings, and baptisms; and supervised youth groups. He gave 16 hours of religious instruction at 5 different levels. People who knew him at the time say he was open, down to earth, and always available. He felt challenged by the work, becoming more aware of

Joseph (right) and Georg Ratzinger were ordained to the priesthood in Munich, Germany, on June 29, 1951. Although the brothers entered the priesthood together, they would take different paths. Georg Ratzinger would become a respected musician and choir director.

the gap between religious instruction and the actual lives of families. As most priests do, he felt bound to the lives of others, alternating between a sense of duty and the pleasure of being part of many lives.

After a year in the parish, his life changed direction yet again. In October 1952, he moved back to academic theological teaching and away from the parish work that had rewarded him with contact with many kinds of people, many of whom were not academics. Although Ratzinger loved serving them, he would never be a parish priest again: He realized he had the temperament of a scholar. As he gained more life experiences, his nature and character unfolded, preparing him for the next phase of his life.

BECOMING A PROFESSOR

Having reached his goal of becoming a priest, Ratzinger began to set other goals. One was to become a professor of theology. In Germany, that goal required two steps: to obtain a doctorate degree and to get an advanced degree called a habilitation. Ratzinger hoped that expanding his essay on St. Augustine would help him win his doctorate, the first step.

He wrote that if he were trapped on a desert island and could only have two books, one would be the Bible and the other would be *The Confessions of St. Augustine.* The story of St. Augustine is one that many Catholic students know by heart. Augustine had a pagan father and a Christian mother, and he came to Italy from his home in North Africa in the fourth century when he was 28. In Rome he became a changed man. The thrill-seeking and hedonistic pagan turned into a charitable and spiritual Christian. He had famously prayed, "Lord, give me chastity, but not yet." He may have been the original reborn Christian, converted in a sudden experience of religious ecstasy. He suddenly saw God as essential to humanity and that God was a part of us and our memory and unconscious. God was a spiritual presence within ourselves for St. Augustine, as well as an objective reality, and we must know ourselves to know God. He also felt that we could

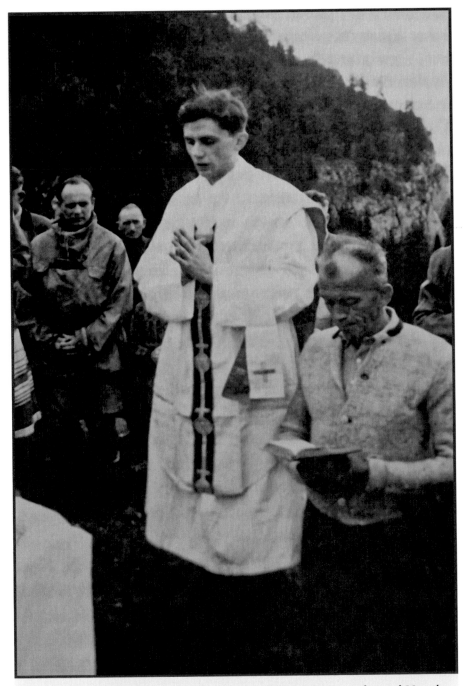

In the summer of 1952, the young priest Joseph Ratzinger performed Mass in the mountains of Ruhpolding, in southern Germany.

see God in this life. Some later popes would disagree, saying that God was hidden from us and we can know nothing about him. St. Augustine did not have that pragmatic view of spirituality. He personalized faith and reserved judgment, criticizing church members who excluded others. He also felt that a congregation could be unified only by liturgy and sacrament. He was an inspiration for Ratzinger then, and continues to be now.

The essay on St. Augustine won Ratzinger a prize and qualified him to take a doctorate exam. The exam had three parts: an eight-hour oral test, a long written test, and a debate on theological issues with experts. Passing with flying colors, he won his doctorate degree in July 1953 in front of two very proud parents. He was ready to take the second step toward becoming a professor, the post-doctoral degree. This advanced degree is a very difficult step, one that only a very few take in Germany. It requires a second dissertation, one that is judged very critically, as well as many hours of coursework. Ratzinger decided to write on Bonaventure, a thirteenth-century saint. St. Bonaventure brought together two parts of the Catholic Church: one part wanted a return to the ways of Jesus, who told his disciples not to worry about tomorrow, but live a simple life; the other part wanted to be practical and plan for the church's future, buying property to build churches and setting up schools to teach the faith. St. Bonaventure found a way to do both, and to keep order in the church. His example was one that Ratzinger would cite often in his views on the role of the church in the modern and changing world.

The two dissertations on St. Augustine and St. Bonaventure represent Ratzinger's best early writing and thinking, and they have some themes in common. Both figures challenged the existing authorities of the church, but both individuals became part of those authorities, working within the church to keep traditions but challenge shortcomings. Both warned about the dangers of the church becoming too political. Both said people must look within themselves for signs of the divine, and to the rituals of the church for the same signs. Both also had another side: they fitted into a tradition that saw sexuality as sinful. From that tradition, misogyny (dislike and fear of women) also springs. The Catholic Church has been influenced by these two powerful figures (and others), and to this day women cannot be priests and priests are required to be celibate. No one knows just how affected the church has been by this strain of thought and belief, but some believe it may be the church's biggest weakness.

While he was writing the second dissertation, Ratzinger lectured in Munich and initially could not devote a sustained period of time to the work on St. Bonaventure. By the summer of 1955, he was able to work on it full time. When he finally submitted it, one of the two scholars judging it gave him a failing grade. This was a blow to Ratzinger that he has remembered vividly for the rest of his life. Historians speculate that the scholar felt that Ratzinger did not pay enough attention to the scholar's own work, thus offending him. Paying proper respect to the work of one's elders and colleagues was very important in this situation, and Ratzinger needed to learn that lesson, the scholar must have felt. He labeled the dissertation "modernist," putting Ratzinger in danger of not reaching his goal of a professorship. However, enough people in the seminary at Freising were familiar with Ratzinger's work that he was given a chance to rewrite the thesis. This tactic was often used by German theological scholars to delay and soften the inevitable rejection. Most in the department assumed Ratzinger would need several more years to complete any rewrite.

Inspired by the challenge, Ratzinger decided he could make the thesis acceptable by cutting some offending "modernist" parts and adding more references to the scholar who rejected him. He knew the literature and scholarship so thoroughly that his rewrite was finished in two weeks, astonishing the readers when he handed it in so fast. His rewritten dissertation accepted, Ratzinger received his advanced degree in early 1957. The two dissertations were so well received that Ratzinger

In his post as a professor in Freising, Joseph Ratzinger lectured to students on dogmatic and fundamental theology.

became an overnight academic star, sought after by the best universities in Germany. However, the experience seemed to radicalize him for a time. A narrow-minded and old-fashioned theologian had almost destroyed his dreams, and he resolved not to become one of those theologians.

A THEOLOGICAL ROCK STAR

In the summer of 1958, Ratzinger became a professor of fundamental theology at the University of Bonn. He was reluctant to leave Freising, where his parents had moved. His friends and his students knew that he could not turn down the opportunity in Bonn, however. Ratzinger was on the way up now, and Bonn was the next step. Bonn is a bustling port on the Rhine River, a melting pot very different from Bavaria. The river symbolized a meeting of many cultures for him. With Belgium and the Netherlands nearby, travelers from all over the world were attracted to spectacular scenic trips down the Rhine. Ratzinger found the city energizing. At night, he could hear the whistles and horns from the river. In Bonn, he made new friends, some of whom were outside theology. This proved to be an important step in broadening his horizons and in becoming more worldly.

Ratzinger was successful as soon as he began lecturing at the prestigious university in Bonn. He may have been only 31, but his lectures were packed to overflowing with eager students who had heard of the brilliance of the new professor. His students noticed that he had the capacity to recall exact quotations at length in various languages. He remembered even the briefest conversations in detail, handled questions from students with ease and thoughtfulness, and impressed his colleagues with his vast knowledge of biblical and theological scholarship. His reputation spread to the townspeople, who often came in before work to hear the beautifully written and clearly delivered talks. These lectures were packed with information and balanced coverage of both meditative spirituality and formal theology. Students were comforted and challenged by his acknowledgement of the distance between humanity and God. They appreciated his clarity about topics that could be very vague, such as identifying which values were most important and when they could be used.

Scholars have noted that Ratzinger is a brilliant formal theologian. For any given theological issue he approaches the problem in a specific way. He starts with the words of Jesus

Christ, then reads all the scholarship about the words, including their historical context and meaning. He then compares
Christian texts with others available and researches all that various Catholic councils, saints, and popes have written about the
words. He finally creates an argument, heavy with footnotes.
The words of the Bible are not enough. For him, God has continued to reveal truths that the Bible's original readers could
not have seen. So, for example, his writing on the Revelation
includes texts by Jewish, Greek, and Catholic writers of all eras.
He reflects on a key to his entire theology: "It is essential to
recognize that the Scriptures are not properly understood when
they are interpreted in a way which contradicts the Church's living tradition." His methods were so thorough, and his research
so extensive, that a theological star was born.

This time of professional gain had personal losses. On a
hot summer day in August 1959, his father suddenly fell ill after
a long walk and died on August 23. Ratzinger was devastated.
Not long after, his mother was diagnosed with stomach cancer,
beginning a long battle with the disease. Ratzinger wrote about
her last days:

> Her goodness became ever purer and more radiant and
> continued to shine unchanged even through the weeks of
> increasing pain. On December 16, 1963, she closed her eyes
> forever, but the radiance of her goodness has remained, and
> for me it has become more and more a confirmation of the
> faith by which she had allowed herself to be formed. I know
> of no more convincing proof for the faith than precisely the
> pure and unalloyed humanity … in my parents.

VATICAN II

Ratzinger's academic brilliance became well known, and in 1962
he made another important step toward his papacy. Surprising
the Catholic world, Pope John XXIII called for a new general
council of the church. General councils are rare and historic

Cardinal Joseph Frings talks to young professor Joseph Ratzinger. Frings would greatly impact Ratzinger's career by taking him along to Vatican II.

meetings with the pope, cardinals, and bishops discussing the future of the church. The First Council of the Vatican had been held in 1869 and 1870, but it was cut short when the Franco-Prussian War threatened Rome. Now, a Second Vatican Council was called; it began on October 11, 1962.

Cardinal Joseph Frings of Cologne, Germany, was a famous biblical scholar, but at 76 he was nearly blind, and he struggled to prepare for the momentous Vatican II meeting (as it was later called). He knew he needed advisors to help him, and no one came more highly recommended than University of Bonn professor Joseph Ratzinger. They met and despite their age difference became immediate friends. Ratzinger would now attend Vatican II as a theological expert advising Cardinal Frings.

Everyone who has studied the results of Vatican II notes that Ratzinger had a great impact on it. Before Vatican II, Catholics had to memorize the catechism, hear the Mass in Latin, keep space big enough for a balloon between dance partners so the Holy Spirit could find a place, and believe that non-Catholics were all going to Hell. None of these survived Vatican II. Catholics could now look forward to hearing Mass in a language they could understand. They could go to an 11:30 A.M. Sunday folk Mass, see *Jesus Christ Superstar*, and not have to worry about their non-Catholic friends' afterlife. They didn't need to be rechristened if they had been baptized in another faith. Vatican II stressed that the Catholic Church needed to be open to the modern world and to other Christian churches, and even to other religions. Religious faith and experience had to be more than reading Scripture. It was in the life of the church, not just in the Bible. Theologians had to have freedom in their research as well. The Second Vatican Council changed the Catholic world, and it changed the way the world looked at Catholics.

Ratzinger was seen as a progressive firebrand, helping push these reforms through. He was now famous in the church as a whole and on an international scale. When Vatican II ended in 1965, he was exhausted, but he knew he and his colleagues had made sweeping reforms. At the end, he must have wondered if too many changes had been brought in too fast. For now, those doubts did not become public.

THE AFTERMATH OF VATICAN II

Joseph Ratzinger had now acted on a world stage and had experienced a taste of having real influence in the church. As he was recovering from his role as expert to Vatican II, many new job offers came flowing in from the great universities in Germany. In 1966, he was recruited by another young theologian rock star of the time, Hans Kung, and took a position at the University of Tubingen. Kung was among the most liberal of the Catholic reformers and believed the church should be engaged in much more political activity. The faculty and students at Tubingen included many who were followers of Karl Marx, who had preached that revolution was inevitable

Noted author and professor Hans Kung was a great influence on Joseph Ratzinger's theological education. However, as Ratzinger became more conservative, they grew apart. Viewed as too liberal for the Catholic Church, Kung's authority to teach Catholic theology has been taken away by the Vatican.

because of the gap between the rich and non-rich. The working poor would overthrow the rich and seize political power, Marx believed. Conflict was good, and it was needed. One Tubingen student wrote at the time, "The revolution was approaching. Our hearts beat faster. Our eyes shone. Our bodies trembled. We were excited, day and night."

Every Thursday night, Kung and Ratzinger had dinner and discussed the great issues of the late 1960s. They were very different people, however. Kung raced around the city in his Alfa Romeo sports car. Ratzinger peddled his bicycle, never going fast enough to knock off his beret. Ratzinger never flirted with Marxism, and he was not as open to complete church reform as Kung. For a time, they were the best of friends and the closest of colleagues. Soon, however, world events would change their view of themselves and each other.

5

The Reformer Reforms

IN THE LATE 1960s, STUDENTS AND OTHERS TOOK TO THE STREETS AROUND the world to protest the Vietnam War and to demonstrate support for civil and human rights. In the United States, campuses from New York to Chicago to San Francisco became intellectual and then physical battlegrounds over the uses and abuses of all kinds of power. In Prague in 1968, Soviet tanks tried to crush demonstrators resisting Communist rule. Students all over began to confront their professors, and many universities had a long series of provocations and responses by radical and conservative forces. Some demonstrations were comic, some tragic.

In Europe, the University of Tubingen was one of the most polarized universities, and Ratzinger was shocked when students distributed a flyer that read, "The New Testament is a document of inhumanity, a large-scale deception of the masses." He asked the students to recall the flyer. They refused and defied him. He

Demonstraters in Prague throw burning torches at an approaching tank in this photograph from August 21, 1968. The late years of the 1960s brought about some of most dramatic and revolutionary world events of modern history, pitting "establishment" against "anti-establishment."

was furious when demonstrators threatened to take over his lecture hall. He feared that the social order was breaking down again, for the second time in his life. He was deeply affected by these challenges to his and other authority. Politics was destroying faith, he felt. He must have feared the worst.

He reacted to the events of 1968 by leaving the university and trying to find a place more peaceful and less radical. In 1969 he moved to a new university at Regensburg, one that would have more conservative students and more restrictions on student demonstrations. Some have compared the move to an editor leaving the *New York Times* for a paper in a small village in upstate New York. But he would also be moving closer to his brother Georg, whom he had missed even more since the death of their parents. This marked a calmer period in Ratzinger's life. He built a house near Regensburg that had the feel of an oasis with a large rose and daffodil garden and a bronze statue of a cat. (Later, the world would learn how much Joseph Ratzinger loves cats.) His sister Maria lived with him, and they were near Georg as well. He called this time "blessed."

In 1970, he published an essay on "The Situation of the Church Today," criticizing intellectuals who equated Christianity with social reforms. Only faith, he wrote, and not reason, will guide us. By 1977 he published two major books, *Introduction to Christianity* and *Eschatology: Death and Eternal Life*. The books have been translated into many languages, and Ratzinger's reputation as a great scholar and writer spread even further. Critics noted that his writing was very clear and pure. The books addressed ways in which great men of the church learn from outside sources yet preserve traditions and social order at all costs. Ratzinger was never as radical as his reputation in the 1960s, and now the world would see this other side of him. To his harshest liberal critics, he was about to go from being a young Jedi knight to a warrior for the Dark Side. His supporters, however, could now envision him as a future world leader. Showcasing his conservative beliefs served to help his career, which effectively spun away from the role of reformer.

RISING WITHIN THE CHURCH

Ratzinger wrote that he had a reaction to the reforms of Vatican II:

> The impression grew steadily that nothing was now stable in the Church, that everything was open to revision.... If the

bishops in Rome could change the faith (as it appeared they could), why only the bishops?… The faith no longer seemed exempt from human decision making…. When I came home after the Council's first session, I had been filled with the joyful feeling, dominant everywhere, of an important new beginning. Now I became deeply troubled by the change in ecclesial climate that was becoming ever more evident…. I tried to sound a first warning signal, but few if any noticed.

In the 1970s, Ratzinger became more conservative. The late 1960s changed him. If Vatican II said church doctrines were open to improvement, he now wanted to slow any more improvements. He wrote that the church is not a "laboratory for theologies." In the early 1960s, he fought the traditionalists in the church. By contrast, in the 1970s, he began to fight the reformers and was rewarded by the church hierarchy for his efforts.

In March 1977, Ratzinger accepted an invitation by Pope Paul VI to become the archbishop of Munich-Freising. It was a remarkable rise from priest to professor to archbishop before the age of 50. Soon after, he became a cardinal. Today the archdiocese of Munich-Freising has some 1,900,000 Catholics, about 60 percent of the region's total population. There are 800 priests and 600 religious men and women in 750 parishes. This is an important position in the Catholic hierarchy, and Ratzinger was able to use his new power almost immediately. Father Abraham Kakkanattu in Chungen, India, had been unable to build a chapel for his parishioners. When he heard of Ratzinger's appointment, he felt he had nothing to lose by contacting him. Within days, he received 20,000 German marks, and the chapel still bears Joseph Ratzinger's name on a memorial plaque for all to see. Increased power meant increased influence on others and a larger network of church friends and allies.

Soon after becoming an archbishop, Ratzinger met a man who would change his life—Karol Wojtyla. The future Pope

Archbishop of Munich and Freising Joseph Ratzinger (right) prays with Bishop Ernst Tewes on March 31, 1977, shortly before Ratzinger's consecration.

John Paul II was a cardinal in Krakow, Poland, and he must have been very impressed with the young archbishop. Germany was looked up to as the gold standard in theological education, and here was one of Germany's golden theologians. Their new friendship would change both their lives. When Pope Paul VI died suddenly in 1978, Ratzinger actively campaigned for his friend to become pope. Wojtyla would not forget his younger friend and ally.

THE INQUISITOR

In November 1981, Pope John Paul II called Ratzinger to Rome and offered him the job of Prefect of the Vatican Congregation for the Doctrine of Faith (CDF). This long title has a long history. The CDF was termed "the Roman Inquisition" when it was founded in 1542 and was charged with stopping the spread of Protestantism, then a dreaded threat to the Catholic Church. The more infamous version of the CDF was the Spanish Inquisition, under Thomas de Torquemada, the father confessor to Isabella and Ferdinand of Spain. He used torture and persecution to punish Jews and Muslims suspected of faking conversion to Catholicism. The methods of torture have been gruesomely detailed in several books, and "the Inquisition" is still in our everyday vocabulary. Ratzinger was always at pains to remind people of the difference between the "Roman" and "Spanish" Inquisitions, and no one knew church history better than he.

The job of head of the CDF in any era is not for the weak of heart, or the meek. Pope John Paul II saw a combative streak in his friend that he thought would be useful in managing dissent by liberal and critical theologians. The job also would be very demanding. Reports land on the CDF prefect's desk every day about happenings throughout the Catholic world—complaints, scandals, sex abuse allegations, and much more. The prefect must decide on a course of action for each, using or setting up binding principles on faith, morals, and conscience, and then imposing them on others. There is some evidence that Joseph Ratzinger disliked the job right from the start and wanted to quit on many occasions. There is other evidence that he grew into the job and became an effective enforcer on many issues.

One of the issues he had to take a stand on immediately as head of the CDF was "liberation theology." Latin American priests and bishops had met in Medellin, Colombia, to support poor and marginalized people in the region. Rich and powerful interests fought the effort to ally the church with the poor, and a few priests armed themselves and joined militant groups like Peru's Shining Path. One of those was Father Camilo Torres, and he was killed for his efforts to help the revolution. Many others were killed or injured as well over a period of years as leftist political movements tried to bring change to Latin America. This was just the kind of tragedy that Pope John Paul II and Joseph Ratzinger feared when politics and religion came together, when church members worked outside the church's authority. For better or worse, Ratzinger was the main force in cutting off support for liberation theologians. On September 3, 1984, he issued an explanation of church law called "Certain Aspects of Liberation Theology," which asserted that liberation theology betrays the poor by locating evil only in political and economic terms. Some felt that the socialism embedded in the liberation theology would have failed the region no matter what. Others felt any movement to help the poor and lessen poverty deserved more of a chance, and that repressive regimes needed to be overthrown. In any case, as head of the CDF, Ratzinger was instrumental in helping silence the liberation theologists.

Another issue that made Ratzinger lose some friends and gain others soon after becoming prefect was his stance on Communism. In 1984, he called it "a shame of our times" and an "illusion." "Entire nations are kept in servitude under conditions unworthy of the human person, while it is claimed they are being brought freedom," he said. This came at a time when the Soviet Union was still strong and the Cold War very much alive. Of course, knowing how much Pope John Paul II hated Communist rule, Ratzinger may have been only amplifying a signal from the pope. Or, he may have been remembering how much the Communists were despised in Germany during the 1930s. In any case, Communist countries reacted with a collective fury at this insult. Pope John Paul II accepted some of the credit for the fall of the Soviet Union in 1989, but Ratzinger

Cardinal Joseph Ratzinger greets Pope John Paul II as the newly elected pope receives German cardinals in the Vatican Apostolic Palace on October 18, 1978. Ratzinger's friendship with the pope helped his career considerably.

deserves some credit as well. Both men grew up in a culture that despised the Communists, and both must have been proud of their efforts in defeating them.

Ratzinger quickly gained a reputation as an enforcer for the pope's doctrines and an effective enforcer at that. People began to notice that friends of the prefect's positions tended to get rewarded. Some of his allies in the fight against liberation theology and Communism rose through the church's ranks more quickly than some opponents. So, a second reputation took hold during these early days as prefect of the CDF: Ratzinger the bold organizational in-fighter. In 1986, Father Charles Curran at the Catholic University of America had said that contraception was not always wrong and that some homosexual relationships should be accepted. Ratzinger had to ask him to deny these positions publicly and when he didn't, Father Curran was asked to leave his teaching position. When

Archbishop Raymond Hunthausen of Seattle withheld one-half of his income taxes on the grounds they were being spent for nuclear arms, he was investigated by the CDF and put through a 13-hour interrogation. He took early retirement soon after.

How much of what Ratzinger did in his role of enforcer was on his own, and how much was carrying out the wishes of Pope John Paul II? Historians will debate this issue for some time. Together the two men made the Catholic Church's position very clear on a number of issues. The strongest statement of the prefect of the CDF's views, and probably the pope's, came in the form of a report that made headlines around the world.

The Ratzinger Report

In May 1985, many of the issues that were swirling around the prefect of the CDF were compacted into a bombshell of a document. *The Ratzinger Report* is actually a series of interviews with Ratzinger, done by Italian writer Vittorio Messouri. The interviewer describes the future pope as "an ascetical person but quite human; he could smile and trade jokes. He went about dressed as a simple clergyman." During the interviews, Ratzinger covers a wide range of issues and makes judgments that continue to affect the church today.

In the report, he says that the legacy of the famous Vatican II needs to be reexamined, that "centrifugal forces" were let loose in the church from that council. He hints that the bishops after Vatican II took too much decision making into their control, and that power sharing between the pope in Rome and the bishops around the world has become imbalanced toward the decentralized bishops. He reiterates that the pope is the descendant of St. Peter and has supreme authority; the bishops are not independent of Rome. The word "power" is seldom heard in any church debates, but the issue of who is in charge of the church, the pope and the curia (administration) in Rome or the local bishops, priests, and nuns, is an issue of

THE REPORT STRESSES ANOTHER THEME, THAT TOO MANY CATHOLICS HAVE AN "UNCRITICAL OPENNESS TO THE WORLD."

force and counterforce that continues to push and pull at the church even today. An institution with the size and scope of the Roman Catholic Church has many internal disputes, but most never become public since the Vatican is a world closed to most media scrutiny.

The Ratzinger Report goes on to declare that there has been a decline in obedience to the church. The faithful are losing a sense of the "mysterious superhuman reality." The fundamental structures of the church are willed by God and should not be open to reformers. Radicals have no right to interfere with centuries of church traditions. Other religions have no right to claim that their faithful are the saved ones. Attacking the problems of today requires that the church use the wisdom of the ages, in texts from the Bible, in passages from the church fathers, and in messages from the past and present popes. Ratzinger's favorite fable is from the Brothers Grimm, known as "Johnny in Luck," in which a master rewards his servant with a large chunk of gold. As the servant walks home, the gold grows so heavy that he has to unload it. He begins to barter: first, he exchanges the gold for a horse, then exchanges the horse for a cow, then the cow for a goose, then the goose for a grindstone, which accidentally falls into a well. He is now free from any burdens. Ratzinger has said that the church had lowered its demands on churchgoers step by step, but that finally the faithful had lost the gold of the traditional church.

The report stresses another theme, that too many Catholics have an "uncritical openness to the world." The general culture is pleasure-seeking and individualistic. Skepticism has infected

Bidding farewell to Munich, Cardinal Joseph Ratzinger walks through a crowd of believers, following a service in Munich's cathedral. Ratzinger left his post in Munich to head up the Vatican's Congregation for the Doctrine of Faith.

even Christian believers, and the truths of the church are offending people. Western culture is hostile to faith. "It is time to find again the courage of non-conformism, the capacity to oppose many of the trends of the surrounding culture."

Ratzinger asserts that the "bond between sexuality and motherhood has been ruptured. Separated from motherhood, sex has ... lost its point of reference." He argues that people have become too open to sexual experimentation, that in retrospect Vatican II let people down by not having enough emphasis on morals, and on self-discipline. Sensuality in the culture at large, he says, has spread to every phase of life and eroded society's ability to raise children who are innocent. People have become too liberated and not free in the deeper sense of giving themselves to Christ and religious love.

In the report he restates the church's position on homosexuality, that it is not a sin but a disorder. He condemns violence or discrimination against gays and lesbians, but he regards opponents of his views as ignorant or undermining. Most homosexuals find this position to be contradictory. It seems to tell them they must choose between their church and their conscience. He also restates the positions that radical feminists have encouraged women to be anti-men and that ordaining women as priests would undermine the church's traditions. In 1994, the CDF would make a definitive ruling against women's ordination.

The Ratzinger Report created quite a controversy. Some wondered how much had been approved by Pope John Paul II and how much was Joseph Ratzinger's personal opinion. The archbishop of Vienna, Franz Konig, challenged Ratzinger and said the church had to move forward, not backward and to the far right. Father Matthew Fox compared the church to a dysfunctional family, where an alcoholic father is appeased so he will not become violent again. Fox left the church to become an Episcopal priest. Hans Kung wondered if his old friend had sold his soul for power.

FINAL YEARS IN THE CDF

Further into his term as prefect of the CDF, Ratzinger widened the scope of his interests and influence beyond the issues in *The Ratzinger Report*. Unfortunately for him, one issue began to dominate in the late 1990s: Rumors and internal allegations about priests sexually abusing young boys exploded into the world media. Ratzinger's most public role as prefect for the CDF came when the clergy child sex abuse scandals became front page news in 2002. The controversies and lawsuits continue to swirl today. Ratzinger did investigate and reopen investigations into several allegations against priests for sexual misconduct. He also declined to pursue several cases, and some believed he was trying to bury the truth about the extent of abuse. The relationship between the American Catholic Church and Ratzinger and Rome became strained almost to the breaking point, and the fault lines are still active. His defense of the church was broadcast around the world:

> In the Church, priests are also sinners. But I am personally convinced that the constant presence in the press of the sins of the Catholic priests, especially in the United States, is a planned campaign, as the percentage of these offenses among priests is not higher than in other categories, and perhaps it is even lower.... The constant presence of these news items does not correspond to the objectivity of the information nor to the statistical objectivity of the facts.

Another issue that gained attention was his strained relationships with some of the world's best-known politicians, including American presidential candidate John Kerry in 2004. A reporter who covered Ratzinger for many years, H.J. Fischer, watched interactions between politicians and the prefect, and wrote, "He could behave with wounding arrogance when he talked to ... clever politicians who wrapped up the pursuit of their own selfish interests in the mantle of Catholic good will.... He knew he was not making many friends among politicians."

Ratzinger continued to be the prefect of the CDF until the death of John Paul II in April 2005. His rise to power took another step when he was named to be the dean of the College of Cardinals on November 30, 2002. His views had served him well, and again he had been rewarded. However, many have oversimplified his role before becoming pope as well as his seemingly unyielding conservative stances. As the years wore on, he seemed to change his enforcer role. He had always had a softer side, even a shyness and a dislike of confrontation. His writing contained many sharp words and pointed attacks, but his conversations rarely did. Despite the reporter's impression previously quoted, he rarely struck people as arrogant. Arrogant people are self-satisfied and uncaring about what other people think. Ratzinger was and is a great listener, according to those who have spent a good deal of time with him.

People who know Ratzinger well say he believes he must defend his faith and the believers who cannot fight back against a hostile culture. Since people are not really protected against those in power, they need the presence of God. Social justice can be fought for, but not at the expense of a belief in the Gospel. He worries that faith will not be preserved for a new generation. He worries that people join the church for a better life before death, rather than for the church's true purpose, a promise of life after death. Ratzinger has described an image from the Danish philosopher Søren Kierkegaard: a priest is like someone dressed as a circus clown trying to warn a village about a fire. The more frantic he becomes, the more people laugh, thinking it all part of an act. He worries that he is becoming frantic in his warnings and that few are listening. He worries that we drown in information and forget truth.

One event that shows the "softer" side of Joseph Ratzinger took place in 2002, when he and Pope John Paul II invited more than 200 religious leaders to Assisi, Italy, home of St. Francis, a peacemaker and lover of the earth and its creatures. There, Buddhists chanted, Shintoists played thin reed instruments, animists from Africa prayed, and John Pretty-on-Top, a Crow medicine man from Montana, smoked a peace pipe. They all gathered at a monastery for pizza, vegetables, Coke, and water. It was a media dream event, the largest interreligious gathering ever held. Pope John Paul II and Ratzinger knew that religious differences can be lethal, and that the differences within their own church needed to be soothed. The gathering opened a period of relative calm within the church.

Another event that shows an evolution away from a strictly enforcer role as prefect, and toward a role he would play as pope, came in March 2000. Leading a penitential service about the mistakes of the church in its 2,000-year history, he admitted the guilt of the church in the violence of the Crusades, the Inquisitions, the silence about Jews during the Holocaust, the failure to respect other cultures and religions, and many more sins and errors. It was literally a humbling experience, and some think it was something the head of the CDF needed to go through before becoming a pope. The reporter H.J. Fischer wrote about Ratzinger during this period:

> [H]e knows how to kindle enthusiasm, to win assent, to provoke objections and contrary arguments; he always succeeds in making me reflect. If I can say that I have sometimes glimpsed the unbending harshness of the Grand Inquisitor, it was in his allergy against all the folly that is spread abroad in the church and the world. Ratzinger saw through everything that was stupid … a cheerful confidence was a core characteristic of Joseph Ratzinger, the man.

CHAPTER

6

The Newest Pope

JOSEPH RATZINGER BECAME POPE BENEDICT XVI ON APRIL 19, 2005.
The pope had joked that being elected to one of the most
powerful and influential positions in the world was like having
a guillotine fall on him. Some observers note that as pope he
has been more conciliatory than he was as prefect of the CDF,
but others noticed that his evolution toward a more unifying
figure began in his later days as prefect. As pope, Benedict is
required to not only judge and monitor, but comfort and save.
He has softened his authoritarian role and reached out more.
He knows that now as pope he must be a center of unity and
not just near the center of power.

Pope Benedict XVI has combined two different styles of
Catholic leadership. One descends from Jesus Christ, who
preached the priority of human needs and caring for others.
The other style is much more authoritarian and is more strict
than nurturing. The pope has much more experience with the

second style than the first, and may never feel he has to balance the two. His predecessor did strive for balance and in the process became a great leader.

THE FIRST DAYS

In his first few days as pope, Benedict reached out to China, approving the consecration of a new bishop in Shanghai. There are no formal relations between China and the Vatican, but this was a start. Pope John Paul II and Joseph Ratzinger helped bring down the Berlin Wall and the Soviet empire. Perhaps Pope Benedict can make a difference in improving China's human rights record.

Pope Benedict made an impact as one of the hosts of World Youth Day in Cologne, Germany, on August 19, 2005. Hundreds of thousands of young people gathered and gave the pope a raucous welcome when he arrived. In a lunch with several young people from around the world, including Chile and the Congo, he talked about the importance of young people in today's world and even did some translating. He waved away a special meal, saying he wanted the vegetable omelet the others were having. He listened to their stories and answered their questions. One of the topics was relativism, one of the new pope's favorite topics. Pope Benedict pointed out the dangers of a relativistic approach that made all moral and religious beliefs equally valid. In a speech to some bishops that day, he went on:

> [T]he young people, with....their enthusiasm in renewing the Church,.... will continue to challenge us. We know that secularism and dechristianization are gaining ground, that relativism is growing and that the influenece of Catholic ethics and morals is in constant decline…. We must accept the challenges of youth, but in turn we must inculcate in young people patience, without which nothing can be found; we must teach them a healthy realism, and the capacity to be decisive.

He met with Muslims on Saturday, August 20, 2005, and told them better relations between Christians and Muslims would be needed to defeat terrorism. Pope John Paul II emphasized the common ancestry Christians and Muslims have through the leader Abraham, but Pope Benedict has taken a tougher stance. He was not shy in pointing out that Muslims bear much of the responsibility for helping to defeat terrorists and that Muslim teachers have to better educate their students against violence and hatred. He said, "Terrorism of any kind is a perverse and cruel decision, which shows contempt for the sacred right to life," and called terrorism "a new barbarism." Whether the pope can help as much in this fight as the previous pope did in the fight against Communism remains to be seen. The stakes are perhaps just as high.

Pope Benedict has also made overtures to Orthodox Christians. In 1054, Christianity was split into two main branches, the Roman Catholic Church and the Eastern Orthodox Church. They have many theological and cultural differences, and many popes have tried over the centuries to reunite them. All have failed. (In 2002, Pope John Paul apologized to the patriarch of Constantinople for the past sins of the Roman Catholic Church, and two years later the apology was accepted.) The new pope has also made overtures to Jewish leaders. However, he has also offended some by not including Israel in his publicly stated list of countries tragically hit by suicide bombers. The pope's office responded that his list of countries hurt by terrorists was not meant to be exhaustive.

THE ONGOING HOT CONFLICTS

The pope will have to deal with many "hot conflicts" and other issues as his term continues. One is the church's ban on contraception. As AIDS spreads in Africa, partly because condom use is low, many public health officials are appealing for a change in the church's position. Allowing Africans or others infected

The 265th pontiff of the Roman Catholic Church, Pope Benedict XVI blesses the crowd from the central balcony of St. Peter's Basilica at the Vatican on April 19, 2005.

with the AIDS virus to use condoms, they argue, would slow the spread of this deadly plague.

Another hot conflict centers around the teaching of evolution. The Roman Catholic Church has tended to stay away from a definite position contradicting generally accepted modern science. However, more bishops have discussed the need for teaching intelligent design, the concept that such a

Pope Benedict XVI poses on the Roman Catholic Church's 20th World Youth Day on August 19, 2005, in Cologne, Germany. The day marked the pope's first foreign trip as pontiff.

complicated thing as life must have a designer. The theory of evolution makes no such claim and says life's complexity can be explained by random processes acting over billions of years. Bitter disputes between and among scientists will continue. Some political leaders in the United States want to mandate that both evolution and intelligent design be taught, to give students a choice. Most scientists counter that science is based on experimentation, and since intelligent design can't be proved through controlled experiments, it is not a science and should not be taught as a science. It instead can be taught as part of several other courses, such as religion, but not as science. In science, miracles are not allowed. Science has nothing to say about why we are here or how we should live, only how the world works.

The rise of fundamentalism in many religions poses some challenges as well. The extremists who seem to have less of a

On June 29, 2005, Pope Benedict XVI bestowed a pallium (woolen shawl) on 32 archbishops from around the world to symbolize their bond with the Vatican. The pope appealed to Orthodox Christians to create a unified, strengthened church.

regard for the loving compassion of God and more for destroying enemies have been called political spiritualists and are a growing force. Some historians says that belligerent righteousness has been a constant temptation for the faithful throughout the long history of God, and that the twenty-first century is as prone to this temptation as any other century. Some have always taken the Bible or the Koran literally, not just seriously. The Catholic Church has tended to take the position that scripture must be read in a wider context.

The Vatican opposed the U.S. invasion of Iraq in March 2003, and Pope Benedict remains committed to this opposition. He must try to engage world leaders in some kind of effective and peaceful diplomacy. President Bill Clinton recalls in his memoirs how often Pope John Paul II would call him and ask for updates on peace talks in the Balkans during the 1990s. Popes have dealt with war and peace for 2,000 years and will continue to do so, almost always promoting peace.

Pope Benedict is not likely to change the church's ban on women becoming priests or allowing priests to marry. He is unlikely to lighten the church rules for divorced and remarried Catholics. He will still, in all likelihood, want all bishops to be chosen by the Vatican and the pope. He is, as we have seen, a student of tradition, and now he is an elected protector of it.

THE POPE'S DAY

Like any pope, Benedict has days filled with events large and small. The pope is as busy as a parish priest but a bit more visible. On any given day, the pope has many meetings, and the Vatican is always a very busy place. The bronze doors on the north side of St. Peter's Square will open early, and a cardinal living nearby will be greeted by the Swiss Guard and let into the Vatican. He will have a weekly meeting in a department of the church government and will need to meet with the pope to discuss recent developments in the writing of the compendium on catechisms. A bishop from Uganda will prepare for a meeting to discuss funding for a new school. In the Apostolic Palace, an assistant to the pope will read some of his daily e-mail, flagging one about an upcoming United Nations conference on respect for human rights. The e-mail will be forwarded to the secretary of state for the Vatican, who must meet with the pope immediately to decide who should attend the New York meeting. A group from the Sisters of the Immaculate Conception in Malta will have an audience with the pope. Other groups will meet with the pope today: the parents of the altar services in St. Peter's Basilica and then several young people on a pilgrimage from Saint Paul's parish in Houston, Texas.

Following a tradition instituted by Pope John Paul II, Pope Benedict XVI baptizes ten newborns at the Sistine Chapel on January 8, 2006. Personally welcoming the church's newest members allows the pope to stay connected with the Catholic people.

A financial aide in one of the palace offices will instruct a bank in Zurich to purchase some Norwegian transportation bonds and will then send a sell order to a brokerage on Wall Street in New York for some energy stocks. A report on the state of the Vatican's financial affairs for the current year will be drafted by another worker, to be submitted to the secretary of state for the pope's information.

In a Vatican library, some pilgrims from Iowa will watch a videotape of the pope's funeral Mass for John Paul II, noting how precise and delicate his movements are. A visitor from Ottawa will pray on his knees outside the Sistine Chapel. A cardinal who is the archbishop of New York will arrive for a meeting with the pope on a development in a high-profile sex abuse scandal involving a priest and a man claiming he was abused when he was 12. An aide to the pope will prepare a private report on the influence of Harry Potter books on the world's young people. Friars from Indonesia will take the palace tour and will also hope to see the pope briefly. A diplomatic party with leaders from Brazil will go off without a hitch in the early evening. The pope will end his day with evening prayers to a large audience that has waited all day for his words.

THE POPE'S LEGACY

Only time will tell what the pope's legacy will be. Is the Catholic Church in a permanent decline or has it entered a new phase of restoring belief in its traditions and rules? Each pope throws himself into a belief in the second possibility, knowing that the church has always been threatened by barbarians, terrorists, war, plague, and persecution. Every pope has had to deal with cultures that lie, and cheat, and steal. Each has known that human nature is both creative and destructive. Each has known that many will always take the path of least resistance and say this choice is a moral principle or what God wants. Each has been in a very special and even dangerous position: each prays for the wisdom to know what is God's will and what

Pope Benedict blesses the crowd at his weekly general audience in St. Peter's Square at the Vatican on October 5, 2005.

is not. People who think they are representing God, and who think they know God's wishes, can be saviors or tormentors. Each pope has known just how difficult a virtue compassion is, how natural insecurity and prejudice can be, and how the church must play a role in instilling compassion through its teachings and practices.

Pope Benedict XVI gives some indications that he will use his power with humility and not assume his own infallibility. He has admitted that religion can be a source of error, as well as a source of civilization itself. He knows that we don't like any limits on our freedom but believes that some limits may save us. The pope has made several references already in speeches and letters to the fact that we must not be afraid. He joked in 1997 that he was "only afraid of the dentist." Those who have watched him closely say he loves celebrating Mass and the liturgy because he knows these symbols of faith and compassion keep us away from an emptiness, a void. He knows more than most popes both the lessons and warnings of religious history, and he will be judged on how much force he can exert for unifying and strengthening the Roman Catholic Church and modernizing its ways without losing its traditions. His papacy will hang in the balance.

One of his most recent speeches sums up his lifelong commitment to faith:

> It is vital to make people understand that faith is permanently up-to-date and perfectly reasonable…. We must not think [of the church] of a pack of rules to be shouldered like a heavy backpack on our journey through life. In the end, faith is simple and rich: we believe God exists, that God counts, but which God? A God with a face, a human face, a God who reconciles, who overcomes hatred and gives us the power of peace that no one else can give us. We must make people understand that Christianity is actually very simple and consequently very rich.

The Catholic Church has survived for a very long time with this simple and rich faith. Catholics have always been able to combine the past and the present to prepare for the future. They draw on the strength of the church, and of the pope. Pope Benedict XVI gives them many strengths to draw on.

CHRONOLOGY

1927   Joseph Alois Ratzinger is born on April 16, in Marktl am Inn, Germany.

1929   Family moves to Tittmoning, near border with Austria.

1932   Family moves again, to Auschau am Inn.

1937   Father retires from police force, and family moves to Hufschlag, outside Traunstein.

1939   Enters minor seminary in Traunstein, St. Michael's School.

1941   Forced to enroll in Hitler Youth but dismissed later because of intention to become priest.

1943   Drafted as a laborer for anti-aircraft unit called Flak, in Munich area.

1944   September 20, drafted in forced labor on anti-tank trench digging. November 20, becomes part of army.

1945   In April, deserts army, returns home to Traunstein. May, captured by Americans and becomes prisoner of war. June 19, released as POW and returns home. November, begins studying for the priesthood in Freising.

1947   Enters Theological Institute at University of Munich.

1951   Ordained as a priest, and delivers first Mass on June 8.

1953   Receives doctorate in theology from the University of Munich.

1959   Begins teaching theology at the University of Bonn on April 15. On August 23, his father dies.

1962   Becomes theological expert for Cardinal Frings at the Second Council of the Vatican.

1963   Mother dies on December 16.

1966   Begins teaching theology at University of Tubingen.

1969   Begins teaching at University of Regensburg in Bavaria.

1977	Named archbishop of Munich-Freising on March 14. Named cardinal by Pope John Paul II on June 27.
1981	Appointed prefect of the Congregation of the Doctrine of Faith by Pope John Paul II on November 25.
2002	Appointed Cardinal-Bishop of Ostia and Dean of the College of Cardinals on November 30.
2005	Elected Pope Benedict XVI on April 19. Formally enthroned as 265th pope during Rite of Papal Inauguration.
2006	Made first "state of the world" address. Added 15 new members to the College of Cardinals.

BIBLIOGRAPHY

Allen, John L. *Pope Benedict XVI: A Biography of Joseph Ratzinger*. New York: Continuum International Publishing, 2005.

Armstrong, Karen. *A History of God*. New York: Alfred Knopf, 1994.

Baumgartner, Frederic J. *Behind Locked Doors: A History of the Papal Elections*. New York: Palgrave Macmillan, 2003.

Cornwell, John. *Hitler's Pope: The Secret History of Pius XII*. New York: Viking Penguin, 1999.

Fischer, H.J. *Pope Benedict XVI: A Personal Portrait*. New York: Crossroad Publishing Company, 2005.

Grafton, Anthony. "Reading Ratzinger," *The New Yorker* (July 25, 2004): 42–49.

Landler, Mark, and Richard Bernstein. "A Future Pope Is Recalled," *New York Times*, April 22, 2005.

Ratzinger, Joseph. *Milestones: Memoirs 1927–1977*. Translated from German by Erasmo Leiva-Merikakis. San Francisco: Ignatius Press, 1997.

Tobin, Greg. *Holy Father: Pope Benedict XVI*. New York: Sterling Publishing, 2005.

FURTHER READING

Allen, John L. *Pope Benedict XVI: A Biography of Joseph Ratzinger.* New York: Continuum International Publishing, 2000.

Armstrong, Karen. *A History of God.* New York: Alfred Knopf, 1994.

Cornwell, John. *Hitler's Pope: The Secret History of Pius XII.* New York: Viking Penguin, 1999.

Fischer, H.J. *Pope Benedict XVI: A Personal Portrait.* New York: Crossroad Publishing Company, 2005.

Grafton, Anthony. "Reading Ratzinger," *The New Yorker* (July 25, 2004): 42-49.

Landler, Mark, and Richard Bernstein. "A Future Pope Is Recalled," *New York Times,* April 22, 2005.

Ratzinger, Joseph. *Milestones:Memoirs 1927-1977.* Translated from German by Erasmo Leiva-Merikakis. San Francisco: Ignatius Press, 1997.

Renehan, Edward J. *Pope John Paul II.* New York: Chelsea House Publishers, 2007.

Tobin, Greg. *Holy Father: Pope Benedict XVI.* New York: Sterling Publishing, 2005.

WEB SITES
Official Web site for Pope Benedict XVI
vatican.va/holy_father/benedict_xvi

Official Web site for the Vatican
vatican.va

Photo Credits

INDEX

ABOUT THE AUTHORS

CLIFFORD W. MILLS is a writer and editor. He earned a B.A. from Dartmouth College, and an M.A. from Boston University, and has edited books at John Wiley and Sons and Oxford University Press. He has authored articles and books ranging from environmental geography to literature to biography. He currently lives in Jacksonville, Florida.

ARTHUR M. SCHLESINGER, JR. is the leading American historian of our time. He won the Pulitzer Prize for his books *The Age of Jackson* (1945) and *A Thousand Days* (1965), which also won the National Book Award. Professor Schlesinger is the Albert Schweitzer Professor of the Humanities at the City University of New York and has been involved in several other Chelsea House projects, including the series *Revolutionary War Leaders*, *Colonial Leaders*, and *Your Government*.